Women's Informal Associations
in Developing Countries

WOMEN IN CROSS-CULTURAL PERSPECTIVE

Sue-Ellen Jacobs,
University of Washington,
series editor

About the Book and Authors

Informal associations among women in developing countries constitute an important source of vitality and integrity for women. This book evaluates the impact of development programs on women's informal associations and sharpens our understanding of them. The participation of women in development via their informal networks presents a dilemma insofar as intervention by development organizations into the informal sphere often forces women to use their associational resources defensively and, at times, even insulates them from development itself. The authors look at credit, labor, ritual, and religious associations; compare structures; describe differences; and assess the capacity of these women's organizations to make use of developmental assistance. They conclude that mobilizing existing associations is often an inappropriate development strategy, and they advise the creation of new associations "by analogy"—using knowledge of informal organizational structures to generate new groups modeled after the old.

Kathryn S. March is assistant professor of anthropology, women's studies, and Asian studies at Cornell University and is a fellow at Mary Ingraham Bunting Institute, Radcliffe College. **Rachelle L. Taqqu** received her MBA from the Cornell Graduate School of Management and has taught at both Stanford and Cornell universities.

Women's Informal Associations in Developing Countries:

Catalysts for Change?

Kathryn S. March
and Rachelle L. Taqqu

Westview Press / Boulder and London

Women in Cross-Cultural Perspective

This Westview softcover edition was manufactured on our own premises using equipment and methods that allow us to keep even specialized books in stock. It is printed on acid-free paper and bound in softcovers that carry the highest rating of the National Association of State Textbook Administrators, in consultation with the Association of American Publishers and the Book Manufacturers' Institute.

Published in 1986 in the United States of America by Westview Press, Inc.; Frederick A. Praeger, Publisher; 5500 Central Avenue, Boulder, Colorado 80301

Library of Congress Cataloging in Publication Data
March, Kathryn S.
    Women's informal associations in developing countries.
    Bibliography: p.
    Includes index.
    1. Women's networks—Developing countries. I. Taqqu,
Rachelle. II. Title.
HQ1870.9.M37 1986   305.4′09172′4   84-19664
ISBN 0-86531-856-5

Composition for this book was provided by the authors.
This book was produced without formal editing by the publisher.

Printed and bound in the United States of America

The paper used in this publication meets the minimum requirements of the American National Standard for Permanence of Paper for Printed Library Materials Z39.48-1984.

6   5   4   3   2   1

Contents

Preface: Making Women Visible

In most parts of the developing world, the major benefits of economic growth have failed to reach women. Women have also paid a steep price for the modest glimmerings of modernity that have reached them. In different places around the world, women's labor obligations have multiplied, their independent resources have shrunk, and their autonomy and cultural worth have often diminished as development has unfolded.

Failure to develop women's resources and skills undermines development as a whole. Women's labor, whether paid or unpaid, is essential. Women everywhere are primary caregivers for their families and children. Decisions women make and skills women have materially affect the health, nutrition, attire, cleanliness and emotional equanimity of all family members. With the sharpening recognition that development hinges on the fulfillment of basic human needs and the quality of life, as well as on the transfer of capital and technology, women have at last found their way onto the international development agenda. (But the resolution of these problems has barely taken shape.)

Effective programs demand accurate and detailed information about what women do: where and how they work, with whom they cooperate or compete; how they help support their households; what resources they control and how they exert that control; in what ways they make or influence decisions and shape community opinion. Existing ideologies about the sexual division of labor, or power, cannot accurately guide the collection of this information. Most recent portrayals of women's lives cross-culturally have in fact differed vastly from assumptions about what women ought to be doing. Conventional wisdom about the powerlessness or passivity of women seldom reflects the patterns of work and structures of authority that actually prevail.

In studying the range in women's socio-political actions and economic contributions, one avenue of investigation has led from an interest in the sexual division of labor to analysis of the household economy as a basic unit of production. Such research, although concerned primarily with women's contributions, converges with an older and recently resuscitated field of economic analysis. Studies of the household economy frequently explore precise patterns of labor allocation within the household and can thus help strip away ideological blinders to women's actual economic contributions at the household and community level. Because such studies often assess the articulation of the household economy to wider economic opportunities and demands, they have the further advantage of placing women's productive and reproductive activities within a larger economic context and of revealing the complementarity of women's and men's roles. Generally, then, their conclusions can be framed in terms of broader policy recommendations.

Parallel to household economics is the growing but uneven field of family studies. Concerning women in development, many family studies have aimed to bring further insights about social values as they are shaped by the family, women's options as the family defines them, and the relationship of both values and options to production patterns. Household and family studies are more or less distinct if overlapping fields of investigation, with the household more rigorously defined as a locus, not for sentiment or kinship obligations, but for production and reproduction. As analytical prisms for understanding social action, both family and household have proved useful, not least because each can also be seen as an important nexus between the economy on one hand and socio-political organization on the other.

As central organizing concepts for understanding the experience or position of women, however, both approaches are insufficient. Neither as a place of work nor as a hub of emotional life is the household or the family the sole site of women's activities or culture. Even if we limit ourselves strictly to women's most tangible, or instrumental, social contributions, an exclusive focus on the household economy will produce an incomplete and distorted picture. It ignores other forms of extra-domestic and extra-familial relationships, which vitally shape women's experiences, and which, in a wide variety of settings, consist largely of single-sex associations. The study of women cross-culturally has shown that women's associations with one another are as important for women as same-sex associations are for their men, and that both types of association typically animate the life of a community. Residual dogmas ordaining woman's place to be in the home should not blind us to these additional sources of social, political, and economic energy.

Anthropologist Maher has dubbed the casual, daily relationships among women the "woman network" (1974). This, she says, is "not some hypothetical web that links all...women in mysterious solidarity, but an institution, like 'kinship' or 'marriage'," that affects most people's lives (1974:53). What Maher has observed in Morocco holds true in many if not most developing areas, including places where the women's world is less segregated than it is in North Africa. Through their associations with one another, women not only develop a shared identity, but they widen their options.

Our aim in this monograph is to explore the informal associations that enlarge and empower the women's world. Such an analysis is an important complement to studies of household and family on one hand, and to investigation of the formal institutional sphere on the other. We have approached this task, first, by examining the nature of informal associations in general. Then, to point to ways of identifying such associations, we seek to uncover and characterize the varied sources of solidarity and bases for association among women in the different settings of the developing world.

Although women's informal associations form the core of rich cultural worlds, we focus on their political and economic functions. This is not to say that all of women's culture represents "a functional grab for power" (Smith 1979) or for resources. As foci for solidarity and group identity, most of the associations we discuss do not just transfer resources or consolidate power. They impart meaning to women's lives and beyond. For the purposes of this monograph, however, we concentrate largely on narrower aspects of women's culture that are most relevant to the process of economic development.

In evaluating the socio-economic contributions of such associations, we use structural criteria to distinguish among them, separating relatively equitable associations from hierarchical ones and differentiating highly bounded groups from diffuse networks. The typology we describe depicts the wide range of variations that exist among women's associations, while also indicating some of the myriad ways that such associations contribute to the well-being of members and their communities. Finally, we examine possible implications of our study for planning development programs or projects. We question whether informal associations can be seen, as families are, as uniformly effective nexus for linkage between local-level activities and central institutions; and we explore the implications of such connections for governmental or agency policy toward women and development.

We begin our study of women's informal associations in developing countries with the premise that women have been invisible because their associations and activities are largely informal. Development planning has fallen into a vicious cycle: armed mainly with a reduced theory of formal organizational behavior, it has been slow to acknowledge the social significance of women in the informal arena. By further modeling planned changes on western paradigms and by equating modernization with formal institution-building, many development practitioners and third world governments have turned faulty observations into self-fulfilling prophecies. In the process, they have hurt both their goals of economic development and political integration, and have further disadvantaged women in developing countries. An understanding of women's informal associations focuses our attention in a different direction and unfolds other possibilities.

Kathryn S. March
and Rachelle L. Taqqu

Acknowledgments

Although final responsibility for this volume rests, of course, with us, and the many individuals who so generously assisted us in its preparation cannot all be thanked, we would especially like to acknowledge:

Jane Kellogg for her extraordinary skill in typing and formatting;
Stacy Leigh Pigg for her careful indexing;
The Center for International Studies at Cornell University for
supporting the original research; and
both our editors at Westview and our future readers for their
patience in waiting for this work to be completed.

K.S.M.
R.L.T.

PART ONE

Women's Informal Associations in Perspective

1

Toward a Definition

LEGITIMACY AND LAW

The contrast between formal and informal is one that most of us understand intuitively but have trouble defining precisely. We instinctively judge, for example, that state bureaucracies, political parties, corporate businesses, and even many so-called voluntary social clubs are essentially formal associations, while the ties of friendship, kinship and many of the bonds between patron and client appear informal.

To establish a definition of informal associations, this chapter focuses on two initial criteria -- legal recognition and organizational structure. We will attempt, first, to render the notion of jural legitimacy more precise by examining some familiar preconceptions about power and authority, and about the presumed greater legitimacy of activities carried out in the public eye as opposed to those which take place in greater privacy. We next investigate the principal structural characteristics of informal associations. The chapter concludes with a working definition of informal associations and also suggests why women's informal organizations play such pivotal roles in developing areas.

Power and Authority

Since formal organizations enjoy explicit legal recognition, they generally are seen as exercising authority and not just power. In other words, formal associations are considered formal in part because of the kind of power that underlies them -- authority that derives ultimately from state institutions. This presumed correspondence between formal associations and legally recognized authority is often taken to imply an absence of authority in informal associations even though it is well known that informal groups can exert power and wield authority. To understand why misconceptions about the informal sphere persist, it is useful to consider some of our assumptions about power and authority.

At its most fundamental, power is the ability to coerce. The powerful are able to impose their own desires, needs, fears, and even fantasies upon the powerless. The basic definition can be embroidered on indefinitely. In some instances, for example, it might be significant that power need not exercise sanctions of actual force in order to obtain its ends. Or, one might wish to elaborate upon the variations found in the sanctions used: physical force, control of necessary economic productive resources, imposition of unendurable emotional or psychological strain, control of the necessities of human life, and so forth. In other instances, it might be important to devise measures of relative powerfulness -- in terms of the numbers of individuals under the sway of a particular power, or in terms of the amount of the force exerted in any direction. In all of these various perspectives, however, the ultimate definitional core remains the same: power is the ability to accomplish one's will regardless of the means employed, up to and including coercion.

Authority, on the other hand, derives from legitimacy. The crux of legitimate authority is that it is exercised with public sanction. It presumes to represent the collective public will and the basis for its claim to power over others lies in the presumption that it expresses that collective will. Whether or not it also has the ability to coerce is a separate matter.

The popular understanding of power and authority, which is tied to our perception of the evolution of formal institutions from informal ones in the west, associates legitimacy with the claims of state institutions. According to Weber's widely accepted social evolutionary schema, with the consolidation of state systems in the west, traditional and charismatic forms of authority were replaced by the 'rational' authority of law and legal bureaucracies. Although Weber himself makes it clear that there are several distinct and legitimate bases for societal authority, his emphasis on the emergence of rational-legal authority within the state has by now colored the very idea of authority. Perhaps because jural-political authority superseded other kinds of authority in our own history, it has largely superseded them in our thinking as well. The historically specific, political-jural form of authority that evolved in the west appears to have come, by itself, to signify the total concept of 'legitimate' authority.

From this perspective, formal associations appear legitimate because they are empowered by rational jural-political charters. The fact that informal associations do not have such charters, however, neither makes them illegitimate nor excludes them from political processes. Public acceptance and sanction, not charters, constitute the primary basis for authority. And public sanction does not always or only find expression in rational jural-political charters, although uncritical usage tends to equate the two.

A Multiplicity of 'Publics'

Conceptual confusion is compounded by a related failure to distinguish between several meanings of the word 'public'. In particular, there are two primary competing ideas underlying our sense of 'public' that must be distinguished: 1) 'the public,' that is, a conception of collectivity in whose name action is undertaken; and 2) 'public' in the sense of 'out in the open,' or not secret, as in the 'public eye.'

In a discussion of women's political activities in West Africa, Van Allen provides an excellent summary of these two aspects of our idea of 'public:'

> One notion of 'public' relates it to issues that are of concern to the whole community; ends served by 'political functions' are beneficial to the community as a whole. Although different individuals or groups may seek different resolutions of problems or disputes, the

'political' can nevertheless be seen as encompassing all those human concerns and problems that are common to all the members of the community, or at least to large numbers of them. 'Political' problems are shared problems that are appropriately dealt with through group action — their resolutions are collective, not individual. This separates them from 'purely personal' problems.

The second notion of 'public' is that which is distinguished from 'secret', that is, open to everyone's view, accessible to all members of the community. The settling of questions that concern the welfare of the community in a 'public' way necessitates the sharing of 'political knowledge' — the knowledge needed for participation in political discussion and decision. A system in which public policy is made publicly and the relevant knowledge is shared widely contrasts sharply with those systems in which a privileged few possess the relevant knowledge — whether priestly mysteries or bureaucratic expertise — and therefore control policy decisions (Van Allen 1976: 64).

The concept of 'public,' then, subsumes two major facets: the nature √ of the collectivity involved, and the nature of the space or style in which that collectivity operates. Van Allen's purpose in distinguishing these two perspectives is to clarify women's involvement in political decision making, but her distinctions serve wider purposes.

In its first sense, public refers to a public or the public. At its widest, it may stand for the entire populace of a society. More narrowly, it may represent some less universally defined group, one affected by the decisions reached in its collective name. Often, however, we tend to forget this multiplicity of publics and assume that there is only one — the widest, most uniform, total public. By representing the people of any given smaller community as a 'public,' as in 'the reading public,' 'the listening public,' or 'the voting public,' we are led to presume that they constitute a relatively undifferentiated whole. All the individuals in a group conceived of as a public appear to stand in more or less equivalent relations to one another, to the collectivity ('the public'), and to the activities of the collectivity. This assumed uniformity gives rise to an idiom of public interest or common welfare which is essential to formal political action. Public action, public power, and public authority, in this first sense of public, are all undertaken in the collective name and serve some hypothetical collective interest of the affected public.

The modern western idea of 'public' includes another aspect as well. It invokes not only the idea of a wide legitimating constituency, but also a sense of the style or location of public action. Public action is undertaken openly, open to public scrutiny, not clandestinely or behind closed doors. From this perspective, the notion of public becomes a question not of constituency but of access. If an organization is to be public in this sense, all of the constituents must presumably have equal access to the information and skills needed in order to participate, as well as to the physical space in which the activities are likely to take place.

In the west, with the emergence of legal rationality as the principal source of political authority, the two denotations of 'public' legitimacy dissolve into a single concept. Law can command public sanction both because it purports to represent the interests of the entire community, and

4

because, as a rational, visible, and openly enacted system, it is theoretically accessible to all members of the collectivity. In this way, the public eye is thought to oversee the public weal.

In social systems where authority is public in both these senses, formal organizations, as legally recognized embodiments of that authority, have appeared more powerful than elsewhere. Representatives of formal organizations who appear before the public eye in their role as delegates, official representatives, or presidents, seem the most visibly powerful. The decisions and activities of public authorities convey an impression of power because, in reflecting the legal authority that lies behind them, they simultaneously affect vast areas of the public (in the first sense), and they are more widely visible, or public (in the second).

Knowledge about the workings of the law, however, has not invariably meant knowledge adequate for participation. Despite the metaphorical accessibility of the rational-legal system to all, laws have always been used to serve the purposes of special interest groups. Weber, for example, noted how rational laws formulated in a universalistic idiom actually arose to protect the European capitalist classes in particular. In the west, the imperfect articulation between these two senses of 'public' sanction has been marked on the one hand by the proliferation of private but powerful interest groups that are well served by the law. On the other hand, there are many solidary clusters of people whose material welfare is not well served by the law, despite their theoretical access to justice. Both kinds of associations are informal since they lack legal recognition. But the access each has to the political process and to the mantle of authority differs diametrically.

In many parts of the world, formal institutional structures are often far weaker and less ramifying than in the properly 'rational' systems that we call 'modern.' Authority emanates not just from the state, or from rational-legal institutions alone. Religion, clan loyalty, ethnic identity, and a wide variety of other traditions are possible sources of legitimacy; and, as Weber noted, conditions of crisis can typically generate yet another legitimating force or idea — one which he styled as "charismatic" authority.

Not all social organizations amidst these competing authority systems are informal, of course. Some organizations, like local political party branches, are recognized by existing public law, while others, like monastic orders, are empowered by different kinds of laws, such as religious ones. The point, however, is that in weak states, considerable power and legitimacy accrue to informal associations by virtue of their accurate claim to be representing a collective weal, despite the fact that they do not necessarily operate in the public eye. Unlike their counterparts in rational-legal and bureaucratic states, informal associations elsewhere in the world can exert legitimate power even when they lack representation in formal state structures.

One obstacle to recognizing the legitimacy of such informal associations is presented by their small size in comparison to most formal organizations. Public authority, as we have said, is predicated on a presumption of wide agreement on its legitimacy, its right to act in the proclaimed shared interest of some collectivity. But collectivities come in all sizes. The idea of universal legitimacy is primarily symbolic. Rarely are projects undertaken which an entire society agrees are equally in the interests of all its public (or publics).

In some situations husbands alone have the authority to reach decisions for the conjugal community. Or senior lineage heads may act with accepted authority on behalf of an entire lineage segment. So, too, the conception of community may extend to the rights of national delegates to impose their interpretation of shared community interest upon an entire nation-state. Although we tend to conceive of only the last of these as an instance of public authority, what has in fact changed in the shift from marital couples to nations is the scope of the community that the acting authority claims to represent. As long as smaller political communities such as, say, local ethnic associations, have the sanction of their whole constituency, their authority is legitimate. Whether or not they align well with the wider political community and state apparatus is irrelevant to this fundamental local legitimacy although it is critical to their wider power.

A second difficulty in ascribing legitimacy to informal associations lies in their less visible, more private sphere of activity. The privacy or secrecy of informal activities is, of course, highly relative, and bears little correspondence to their public acceptability, legitimacy or power. The problem springs not so much from the privacy of informal associations as from the implications of privacy and private space.

In the west, private space is commonly conceptualized as the opposite of public space: while the latter is equally open to all members of the public the former is closed to all but intimates. Egalitarian ideals of the accessibility of public institutions are matched by parallel expectations that private spaces and personal information are sacrosanct. It is not only that all citizens should have equal access to their public institutions, but those institutions should not infringe upon the individual's right to privacy. Whatever their merits as a system of values, such ideas should not distort observations about the uses of public and private space in other cultures. Legitimacy and political efficacy can derive not only from nationally acknowledged laws but also from more narrowly defined identities.

Informal associations, in sum, do not have legal recognition, but this does not exclude them from political, economic, or social processes. In many third world settings, informal associations have both power and considerable legitimacy, at least within the community of interest they encompass. We recognize this readily with respect to powerful behind-the-scene interests or pressure groups; but, even among relatively powerless groups such as rural-to-urban migrants or women, informal associations regularly play an influential role. This is true despite the fact that informal associations tend to be smaller and less visible than formal associations: their legitimacy hinges on the sanction of a public, not on its locus or size. This is true even though informal associations are rarely as prominent or visible as formal organizations. An exaggerated sense that private or informal life is personal and hence apolitical -- especially among the poor and the powerless — obscures the legitimacy of associations that are not constituted through rational-bureaucratic and legal charters. Viewed in this light, communal sanction is as definitive for informal associations as legal recognition is for formal ones.

STRUCTURE OF FORMAL AND INFORMAL ASSOCIATIONS

Hierarchy

Perceived differences between formal and informal associations also depend on conceptions of group structure. Most informal associations involve fewer hierarchical levels. Some of those levels are often quite broad, creating a relatively flatter hierarchical pyramid than those found in most formal associations. It does not necessarily follow, however, that there are no hierarchical relations, or that all authority within informal associations is exercised in an egalitarian fashion. Patron-client relations are a good example of informal relations that are quite hierarchical but involve few levels, perhaps as few as two — that of the patron and client in direct association.

To a considerable extent, it is the face-to-face nature of informal associations that blurs hierarchies of authority within them. Most informal associations operate, and perhaps are even held together, through direct personal communication and interaction. This direct contact softens the perceptions that participants themselves may have about inequalities within their association. Sometimes it may allow even hierarchical informal relationships to be couched within an idiom of interpersonal equality and mutual obligation. Patron-client ties among women, for example, may explicitly emphasize their shared female experience, although power within the relation is clearly asymmetrical.

On the other hand, a simplistic, and widely criticized, assumption about formal organizations is that they are clear hierarchies of authority.[1] This assumption bears little resemblance to reality, for many complex hierarchies do not incorporate clear channels of authority. This is particularly true in more organic hierarchies: in a kindred, for example, the various families constitute semiautonomous subsystems; they are interconnected at different 'higher' levels of kin organization, but the lines of authority are not always clear. In fact, most complex social systems articulate different subsystems hierarchically without sharply delineated hierarchies of authority. Even businesses and bureaucracies make many decisions which do not follow the routes suggested by idealized hierarchies of authority. In practice, lines of command, even in systems which are structurally hierarchical, are rarely unambiguous. Gaps within or around the edges of formal organizations can allow latitude for informal social relations to exert their influence. Within businesses, families, or bureaucracies, informal social ties cross-cut formal lines of organization and often alter the directional flow of authority.

Hierarchy, to be sure, remains an important structural characteristic that distinguishes formal from informal associations. Formal associations tend to be complex and hierarchically organized, to assign relationships that are based on the positions and role of participants within the organizational pyramid, and to represent themselves as hierarchies of

---

[1]For a more complete discussion of the points here summarized about hierarchy, see Simon (1969).

authority. Informal associations are flatter and tend to involve people in face-to-face, 'primary' relationships in which asymmetries of authority or power, though real, are often masked. It would be misleading, however, to depict the two types of associations as diametrically opposed; they are, instead, relative categories. Conceptually, it is possible to place formal and informal associations along a continuum. At one end of the scale lie the formal associations that most closely approximate organizational hierarchies of authority. Loosely organized and highly flexible associations, at the opposite pole, are often cast in an egalitarian idiom.

Personal Networks

The loose and relatively flat structure of informal associations, together with the face-to-face quality of relationships, often indicate membership patterns that are too variable to demarcate sharply bounded groups. Many of these are best described as ego-centered social networks, made up of dyadic relationships between individuals.[2] The content of these relations can vary enormously -- kinship ties, neighborliness, commitments for the exchange of labor, gossip circles, information circuits, and patronage bonds are some of the many possible examples (Barnes 1954; Mayer 1966).

Representation of informal relations as networks has many advantages. The first and most apparent comes from the admissibility, within a single descriptive framework, of not just one but several key structural positions or nodes -- leaders, decision makers, power brokers, and other influential individuals. Because the representation of networks is not rigidly pyramidal, it is possible to conceive easily of several individuals competing for autonomous spheres of influence that are not readily ranked hierarchically. More strictly hierarchical representations delineate clear subsystems connected through a single link to a superordinate unit. While it is possible to substitute one individual for another at different levels, or in different 'offices,' it is difficult to represent a flexible array of shifting alliances or a multitude of only minutely differentiated levels. From the perspective of networks, however, shifts in leadership, membership participation, and group foci can be discussed explicitly within the organizational framework of the association.

A second advantage of the concept of networks lies in emphasizing the content of the links between individuals within the association. In a hierarchical organization the relations between individuals are assumed to be at least partially relations of authority; in social networks they are not. Instead, the number of contacts drawn through any single individual suggests spheres of influence, or pivotal locations in the communication process, without explicitly attributing power or authority.

---

[2]Here, of course, 'ego-centered' does not imply selfishness: it is a term describing the way in which personal networks are built out around single individuals by establishing one-to-one (dyadic) ties with other individuals.

Purposes

The nature of the bonds between individual participants as well as the great flexibility in both leadership and membership permit such associations to be extremely responsive to changing or unpredictable circumstances. Such associations are capable of expanding or contracting their web of influence. The ties that bind individuals into an informal association lie latent until there is specific cause to activate the network of affiliations, obligations, debts, and demands. It is difficult to consider informal associations without considering the reasons around which any specific informal association has crystallized.

'Purpose' within informal associations can be seen generally to be directed along two vectors. Because, as we have indicated, the structure of many informal associations is defined by personal networks, the personal charisma of key individuals can be crucial. Some informal associations may be the result of the inspiration, energy, and magnetism of the central individual. That individual has considerable personal power over others — as a religious leader over devotees, a patron over clients, elite over non-elites, social senior over juniors, and so forth. Obviously, the bases for such personal appeal are diverse, ranging from personal spiritual devotion to coercive economic disparities. Sometimes these bonds alone are sufficient to mould an informal association.

Individual personalities are not usually the sole force behind informal associations. The presence of effective leadership undoubtedly affects informal associations but it is not a sine qua non. To say that informal associations often take the form of personal networks does not mean that they essentially serve the purposes of the central persons involved. Personal charisma more often serves than is the purpose behind any given informal association.

The more crucial vector defining informal association 'purpose' is membership need. Even in the presence of strong leader magnetism, informal associations rarely cohere unless they fulfill definite functions for the participants. Informal associations respond to specific needs and are mobilized around specific activities. Such activities may be as basic as companionship and child-care exchange, or as specialized as cooperative marketing and pilgrimages. Members usually participate because they want the services that the informal associations organize. Because many informal associations respond to several needs and perform several functions simultaneously, this rather obvious proposition can be easily obscured. Even neighborhood gossip circles, friendship groups, and visiting networks can be mobilized to serve important social and economic needs. As long as the need exists, the activities will continue, and the informal association persists. Depending upon the urgency of the need, the informal association can expand or contract membership and activities accordingly.

THE PROBLEM

Informal associations must be imagined not as the opposite of the pristine organizational forms resembling planned, public hierarchical bureaucracies of authority. If informal associations are conceived only as what formal associations are not, informal may come to denote the powerless, amorphous, unpredictable, privatized schemes for the pursuit of personal ends. Instead, informal associations are structured following independent principles, which are neither imperfectly like nor perfectly unlike the principles structuring formal organizations.

First, informal associations lack legal recognition. But the collective acquiescence of their constituency animates them and accords them legitimacy. Second, informal associations have a more diffuse structure than formal associations. Their boundaries, membership, and hierarchies are less distinct. What both these criteria for informal associations underscore is the significance of the content of informal relationships. It is hard to imagine informal associations without considering the basis and purposes of the relationships within them. We cannot speak of the organization of informal associations without addressing the ongoing who, why, and how of association.

The principles underlying informal associations admit different sources of group strength. Their vitality derives from their flexibility in leadership, membership, and purpose. Leadership can be diffuse or focused, individual or collective, spontaneous or traditional. Membership can be small and tight, large and scattered, expanding or contracting, interrelated in many ways or connected only through involvement in the informal association. Informal associations can be structured about a single specific purpose or they may fulfill many functions simultaneously. What is more, the flexibility of informal associations allows for dramatic shifts in these different characteristics within a single association over time. The same association may initially fulfill one purpose -- say, that of a social dance association -- but then be transformed to serve completely different needs — of a rotating credit association, for example.

The flexibility of informal associations is the source of both their elusiveness and their appeal in planning development. Informal associations, which arise in response to unfulfilled or widely fluctuating needs, stake out a vast domain of social, economic, ideological, and political experimentation. Included in the worldwide record of informal associations is a vast repertoire of organizationally innovative responses to human needs. Yet the fundamental contradiction between the organizational strengths of informal associations and the typically rigid structure of development interventions is inescapable: to reach from the one into the other will not be an easy task.

2

Women's Informal Associations

PUBLIC VERSUS PRIVATE

Within the informal sphere, associations among women have been particularly misunderstood, further clouded by a layer of misconceptions about gender differences. When they have been seriously studied at all, they have been viewed as part of a private, domestic world that is dissociated from politics and public purpose even though it may be seen as preserving the social basis for political consensus. Not only are women's informal associations conceived as personalized and devoid of public authority, even more than informal associations in general, but women's informal connections have been imagined as divorced from the political process itself.

Even network analysis, the primary method for confronting and analyzing the influence of the informal arena, has a curious tradition for treating women, presuming that women participate in few networks in comparison to men. Boissevain, for example, reverts to the tired suggestion that women's bonds with one another are weakened by feminine efforts to attract male attention: a good-looking woman, he postulates, will have fewer close ties with other women than a woman who is not sexually appealing (1968).

The one place where women's participation in social networks has been systematically studied has been in the sociology of the family. Following Bott's initial investigation in 1957, discussion has centered on the nature of the social networks of married couples, and the impact of network structure on the people concerned. This line of analysis, as Banck has written, is an "offshoot of the Durkheimian quest for solidarity and consensus" (1973: 40-41). It has seen social network structure, with its consequent influence on the individual, as a major source of social control.

In the field of political sociology, another area that has relied on network analysis, the treatment of women is relatively casual and coincidental. In game theory and interaction theory, social control becomes a mechanism to be evaded or manipulated by enterprising individuals. The guiding aphorism , according to Banck, shifts from 'Birds of a feather flock together' to 'Politics make strange bedfellows' (1973). Only rarely do network analyses of this type suggest that women may systematically assume specific roles in creating or maintaining networks. In other words, women's networks are rarely recognized as powerful or authoritative except where they reinforce conservative consensus. Such studies emphasize women's passive traditionalism even though their subject is social power and control.

Exploration of women's informal associations thus requires further confrontation with distorting preconceptions. Interestingly, it is the very biases that have diminished the informal sector in general that have doubly slighted women's informal associations. These biases stem chiefly from the prevailing confusion about the meaning of public, and a naive but common extrapolation from western experience. Both find expression in the theory that segregation of men and women into public and private domains is the key to understanding women's subordination to men.

Rosaldo's early observations remain the most succinct summary of this point of view:[1]

> I have tried to relate universal asymmetries in the actual activities and cultural evaluations of men and women to a universal, structural opposition between domestic and public spheres. I have also suggested that women seem to be oppressed or lacking in value and status to the extent that they are confined to domestic activities, cut off from other women and from the social world of men. Women gain power and a sense of value when they are able to transcend domestic limits, either by entering the men's world or by creating a society unto themselves. Finally, I suggested that the most egalitarian societies are not those in which male and female are opposed or even competitors, but those in which men value and participate in the domestic life of the home. Correspondingly, they are societies in which women can readily participate in important public events (1974: 14).

According to Rosaldo's formulation, women's power is limited because their authority rarely extends beyond the limits of small family units, and even within them it is usually circumscribed by cultural norms and often legal strictures. She argues that sexual equality is promoted both by involving men in the domestic sphere and by drawing women out into public life. When the men's authority is invested along with women's in family and household, and the women's embraces the wider community, according to Rosaldo, the legitimacy of both sexes' power is more nearly equal.

Part of the approach outlined in Rosaldo's theoretical overview involves looking at societies where domestic and public domains are not sharply delineated to see how widely women profit from an overlap between these two domains. Sutton and Makiesky-Barrow (1977) claimed that such an overlap is responsible for the relatively greater sexual egalitarianism they report in Barbados. In looking at !Kung Bushmen society in both its traditional context as a foraging society and in the process of change toward an increasingly sedentary way of life, Draper (1975) showed that sexual egalitarianism was greater when they were foragers, partly because the work spheres of men and women were less segregated.

---

[1]Even though Rosaldo later re-formulated her own contrast substantially (1980), it has had far-reaching effects on other writers.

Sanday (1974) specifically pursued the basic question of women's involvement in public activities. She attempted to develop a general model to explain the relation between women's status and their public participation. Her model, which was fully consonant with Rosaldo's, examined the relative contributions of the sexes to three aspects of human activity -- reproduction, subsistence, and warfare. Sanday's model assumed that there is an overall sexual pull which tends to draw men into warfare and women into reproduction-related activities. It was in the relative contributions of the sexes to the middle area, subsistence production, she argued, that the balance of sexual power was determined.

This distinction between public and domestic (or private) spheres has been utilized widely in cross-cultural studies of the position of women. It can, however, be evoked too casually. The public-private distinction is not one simple dichotomy but subsumes several separate, if interrelated, distinctions.

Some of the earliest proponents of the domestic-public polarity have themselves suggested an important initial revision. They have argued that the two spheres are not necessarily hierarchically related, and that we have underestimated the importance of women's domestic powers. More than ten years ago, Netting (1969) spoke of "women's weapons" in domestic politics, showing how women's right to control their own productivity, labor and income, along with certain marital and sexual rights, gave women substantial autonomy, and even constituted a threat to myths of male prerogative among the Kofyar. In an early theoretical piece, Friedl (1967) argued that women's underlying domestic authority and the importance of women in interpersonal community interactions were the "reality" behind "appearances" of male privilege in Greece. Her perspective is advanced by more recent research such as Cronin's on Sicily (1977), or Rogers' description of the "myth of male dominance" (1975).

Other researchers, too, have emphasized the importance of women's domestic contributions by focusing on the economic productivity of the domestic domain. They underscore the extent to which western value assumptions are carried into descriptions of non-western situations. It can be (and has been) argued not only that women's domestic labor is essential to the smooth functioning of whole economies, but that it is uniquely essential in economic systems where women's work remains unpaid, as it is in the west. In such economies, women constitute a great pool of reserve labor, contributing most of their labor to the household freely, and entering and withdrawing from the paid labor force according to the needs of the wider economy. In economic systems such as these, women's domestic labor is doubly devalued: it is neither paid nor recognized as labor. In understanding the economic contributions of women within different forms of economic organization, we must ask whether these also devalue the domestic labors of women or not.

A reconsideration of the value of women's domestic labor also requires reconsideration of the basis for the distinction between domestic and public. There are two related issues here: first, whether political events need always be conceived only in reference to a widely based public or whether political action can be undertaken in the name of smaller-scale constituencies; and, if it can, whether the small-scale economic and political events of the 'private' domestic sector are systematically related to wider societal politics and economies.

14

A number of studies have focused on the first question: whether there is a true domestic politics. They have tried to show that public and private do not represent two discrete kinds of social units, the former society-wide and the latter restricted to small family units. Instead, they attempt to demonstrate that authority can be legitimated by a variety of constituent social groups important to women. Those groups may be very small, as in the uterine family consisting of a woman and her children described by Wolf (1972) in Chinese families of rural Taiwan. Wolf also looks at how the bonds formed between unrelated women who have all married into the same village result in an influential women's community within an otherwise male-oriented society. Lamphere (1974) looks at ways in which women consolidate wider social bases for influence within and between domestic groups. She shows how extended kin links and links connecting unrelated women can be activated, especially to meet the demands of women's domestic labors. Schlegel (1970, 1972) compares the patterns of authority, alliance, and autonomy of women in matrilineal societies to show that the scale and interdependence of women's political constituencies can shift considerably. This line of reasoning parallels some of our arguments about informal associations in general. It suggests that neither the size of a constituency nor its physical location determine its authority.

In a similar vein, other studies extend the investigation of domestic politics to show how women's domestic roles in households can actually widen their political base, sometimes beyond that of men. Strathern (1972), for example, discusses at length the special position of women who move at marriage from their natal community into the communities of their husbands. Because of information they gather in their separate domiciles, these "women in between" become important mediators between men's local lineage groups. The ties binding women to natal and marital groups are simultaneously the ties which also bind localized men's lineage communities into a wider political society. In this Mt. Hagen setting of Highland, New Guinea, it would be plainly absurd to characterize 'domestic' relations as private, apolitical, or devoid of authority.

Many observers of the Middle East have also argued for a conceptualization of women's social and political base as a broad one, uniting domestic group to domestic group and thus actually creates the larger political fabric of the society. Nelson (1974) summarizes a number of ethnographic reports to show how crucial are the bridges that women's constituencies form between male-defined groups in Middle Eastern societies, in spite of women's dramatic segregation into a domestic-private sphere. Nelson cites Peters (1966) to underscore this point:

> The pivotal points in any field of power in this, a superficially dominant patrilineal, patrilocal and patriarchal society where the male ethos is vulgar in its brash prominence, are the women. What holds men together, what knots the cords of the alliances are not the men themselves, but the women who depart from their natal household to take up residence elsewhere with a man, and who, in this critical position communicate one group to another (Nelson 1974: 555).

Women's dual allegiance to marital and natal homes makes them vitally and personally interested in the maintenance of effective political relations between localized male groups. Although women's ties stem √ from what we would identify as the private domestic spheres of natal and marital families, they become publicly political as they unite one private domicile to another. In all these cases, then, women's associations reflect the collective interests and wills of groups of varying size and basis. They are not typified by small-scale families in segregated domestic units alone, but may involve much larger groups.

The position of women in marriage exchange networks suggests additional avenues for extending political constituencies. Throughout Africa, 'wife-giving' and 'cattle exchanges' as strategies for political alliance have long been recognized. In many instances, however, it is not only men who play a role in arranging women's marriages and cementing them with the exchange of livestock. Women, too, through sponsorship of girls' initiation groups, obtain the right to suggest or promote the girls' marriage prospects. Madam Yoko, in Hoffer's study (1974), was able in this way to consolidate an extensive political following. In a similar manner, the various notable African queenships like the great Rain Queen presented by the Kriges (1943) manipulated hundreds of marriages, using a domestic kin-based idiom to establish political networks uniting their hundreds of thousands of subjects.[2] These studies confront not only the degree to which women's associations transcend domestic groups but also the extent to which such groups may have explicitly political purposes and not just domestic economic ones.

This brings us to the second question: the systematic connections between small-scale domestic economies and wider societal politics. Tiffany (1979) outlines a variety of actions, usually taking place in what √

---

[2]Nor were women restricted to arranging the political marriages of others. As Hoffer pointed out,

> Both men and women gave gifts to supporters, the gift being a tangible symbol of a special relationship in which the political aspirant may later ask for a reciprocal favor. Women candidates may give, or at least suggest the bestowal of, sexual favors to a key figure, a political ploy more useful to women than to men. In some cases a woman may bear a child fathered by an influential person, and as the woman ages and diminishes in physical attractiveness, the child remains as a focus to bind the affective allegiance (1974: 174).

Women, then, may have the option of arranging their own marriage(s) and/or sexual alliances in some cultural contexts, binding allies through direct conjugal and co-parental affection. In some African cases, too, women were able to marry other women, even polygamously. In such cases (see O'Brien, 1977), the position of a woman in marriage politics could become almost exactly like that of a man engaging in the taking and giving of wives to create large political constituencies directly, with one great proviso: she also had the potential to bind others to herself personally, either through her own sexual relations or through motherhood. In the Krige study of the Rain Queen mentioned above (1943), for we would call the private-domestic sector, which nevertheless must be construed as overtly political. She reexamines women's control over hospitality, aspects of the supernatural such as personal pollution, sexuality, and even threats of suicide to show that actions undertaken by women within the private domain are political. In particular, Tiffany emphasizes the importance of women's control over the flow of information between men's local lineage groups. In their relations with other women as well as with men of both marital and natal communities, then, women appear to be engaged not just in domestic economies but in political activity which, although originating in the women's segregated private sphere, nevertheless has much wider political ramifications.

Many of the points raised by Tiffany have been discussed by other authors for numerous and geographically dispersed societies. Brown (1975) indicates that one of the main sources of Iroquois women's power may have derived from their ability to control food distribution. In many traditional societies, the profferment of hospitality and exchange of food are not purely domestic or simply convivial activities but, rather, are the stuff of major political events. Among the Iroquois, for example, as Brown shows, those wishing to convene a political tribal council meeting had to provide the food for all participants, food which had to be obtained from the matrons of longhouses — the 'domestic' productive units. Similarly, both Iroquois war efforts and trading ventures were contingent upon senior women's willingness to provision warriors and traders. In such ethnographic cases, it is difficult to extricate domestic economies from community politics.

In Melanesia as well, both Strathern (1972) and Weiner (1976) have shown that men's formal politicking depends upon women's 'domestic' economic contributions. Without the wherewithal of women's productive efforts, men cannot aspire to the kinds of exchanges essential to establishing oneself as a 'Big Man' in the Melanesian form of politics.[3] Moreover, as Weiner's more recent work makes clearer than Strathern's initial efforts did, men are not able simply to expropriate the fruits of women's domestic labors for their public political endeavors. Rather, public politics results from the interweaving of the private productivity and exchange aspirations of both sexes. Such patterns are repeated over much of the globe; relations forged by women outside of formal public politics, whether on the basis of women's kinship or residential connections or because of ties emerging from the labors of their domestic economic sphere, are essential to wider public politics.

---

example, in addition to arranging the marriages of others, the Rain Queen herself had numerous wives but was succeeded in office by her own natural daughter. Although we tend to think of the bonds of motherhood, marriage or siblingship as primarily intimate and private commitments, it is clear than in many societies they provide the basis for allying large political constituencies. (See Chapter 5.)

[3] See also Vincent (1967) for wives' support, through beer-making, of husbands' political efforts.

As this review of the literature suggests, ethnographic evidence does not uniformly support an inference of a sharp separation between domestic and public space. Depending upon local social and cultural traditions, in many parts of the world small-scale markets, local shops, temples and churches, fountains, gardens, and fields are public sites in which women can be found readily, at least at certain times of the day. It requires increasingly great leaps of imagination to delineate distinct private domestic spaces when we consider even less complex societies.

Even in those societies where there is an emergent sense of privacy, and where women's interactions or occupations, if not their literal space, men, women's activities often draw together a distinct women's community. Women from several conjugal units or domestic households often meet, interact, and work cooperatively at their domestic labors. What is private about a public fountain where women draw water or wash clothes for domestic use? There is an important distinction between 'private' in a are segregated from literal, spatial sense, and the possible emergence of separate public spheres for men and women.

Rarely, then, are the presumed functional specializations of public versus domestic groups as divergent or discrete as early analyses reported. Although domestic households are significant units of economic production and consumption in many societies, they are rarely the only important economic units, nor are they apolitical. Women's control over domestic production often gives them considerable influence, even power, and sometimes authority, over the shaping of public political events. Similarly, men's control over formal public politics can alter and constrain the productivity of the domestic domain considerably.

If the distinction between domestic and public is fraught with all these inconsistencies, how did it come to have such importance in the literature on women's position in other societies? The dichotomy between public and domestic arose in the first instance as an observation about the different ways that men and women used space. Reiter has referred to this as "domainance," saying:

> There is a sexual geography to the way people use space within the village as well as outside of it....Public places like the village square, the cafes and the mayor's office are the domain of men, while private places such as houses and the back streets that connect them into residential neighborhoods belong to women (1975: 256).

This interpretation of the public-private distinction is modeled on extreme cases of segregated, enclosed domestic compounds for women, such as are found in many parts of the Middle East and South Asia. The concept, however, has been extended to include a wide variety of other ethnographic instances of less stark spatial segregation of the sexes. Sexual segregation may be temporal as well as spatial, as Reiter indicates: "Not only do men and women use different space in different ways, but they use it at different times as well" (1975: 257). In the case she describes, the street, cafes and the village square belong to men most of the day and evening. But "when the men have abandoned the village for the fields, the women come out to do their marketing in a leisurely fashion. The village is then in female hands" (1975: 257).

But the public-private distinction has been grossly overstated. Women's habitation of private space has been understood not just as isolation from public places, but also as their exclusion from public -- or political -- affairs. In other words, the separate denotations of 'public' that were discussed earlier once again dissolve into a single idea. This confusion, as we have seen, is an outcome of the historical privatization of the domestic domain in the west -- and the corresponding identification of public affairs as the domain of the state. The vision of isolated domestic households that underlies many of our assumptions about the domestic-public distinction probably derives more from the history of our own private sector than from cross-cultural experience.

In the west, there is little doubt that the privatization of women's activities has trivialized those activities and transformed the domestic domain. As women and their contributions become increasingly removed from even a women's public domain, women may become isolated from the larger society and ultimately from one another. Under such circumstances, domestic tasks come to replicate one another within the separate confines of each woman's household. Women's domestic role becomes a supporting role without explicit recognition outside of the privatized household. It would be impossible to consider women in the industrialized west without looking at the triple foil of domestic privatization: physical marginalization, economic devaluation, and social deprecation.

Rapp has styled the public-domestic contrast as it has emerged in the west as the difference between actions motivated by love and those done for money:

> The distinction between private and public corresponds to the distinction between love and money -- one is normatively the subject of the woman-centered family, the other is the focus of male-centered economic activities. We experience those domains and activities as distinct, but, of course, they are interpenetrating. Without secure economic relations ('money'), the households in which nuclear families are expected to live (for 'love') are hard to form and keep functioning. It is women's job to mediate the contradictions between love and money in the private domain...

> We cannot write an accurate history of the West in relation to the Rest until we stop assuming that our experiences subsume everyone else's. Our public/private conflicts are not necessarily the same as those of other times and places...We must simultaneously understand the differences and the similarities, but not by reducing them to one simple pattern (1979: 510-511).

Although it is essential to recognize the impact of these processes where they have occurred, we must remain cautious about inferring the privatization of women's domains in parts of the world where that has not, or not yet fully, happened. We cannot assume, as did Parsons and Bales, that husbands are everywhere primary breadwinners "whereas the wife is primarily the giver of love" (1955: 151). Otherwise, it will remain difficult for us to understand widespread patterns of child-sharing, adoption and caretaking, arranged marriage, polygamy, dowry or bride-wealth, food preparation, lack of conjugal privacy, and a host of other arrangements -- all of which are based upon different assumptions about the location of public and private economies, about restricted and generalized exchanges, or about personal rights and collective obligations. Cross-culturally, both the line between public and private domains and the consequent definition of those domains are much more flexible than western experience would suggest. Neither 'haven' nor 'heartless world' (Lasch 1978) are universal features of the ethnographic record.

It is precisely this exaggerated perception of the jural-political sphere as distinct that has led us to minimize the informal sectors in general and to discount women's relationships in the 'private' realm in particular. Few societies, however, consist only of small isolated domestic units on the one hand, existing within the overarching society as a uniform entity on the other. Even our own does not. Any opposition between nuclear or uterine families in the private domain and the entire community in the public domain is mitigated by numerous intermediate and intervening groupings.

Once 'public' is conceived not as the self-contained domain of formal political institutions but as an arena of collectively sanctioned activity, it becomes apparent that many associations, which span public and private space, also provide women and men with important vehicles for power. The collective sanction that lies at the root of informal associations is therefore a key to the range, pattern, and power of women's informal associations in a specific setting. The more widely the bases for women's associations are accepted, the greater is the constituency that regards them as legitimate, and the broader their power base and potential impact.[4]

DESCENT-BASED CONSTITUENCIES

In their fully elaborated detail, the bases for women's legitimate solidarity throughout the world are bewilderingly diverse. Providing a comparative framework to embrace all that detail, and still preserving the integrity of all the independent collectivities involved, is an audacious task. The analysis is complexly layered, with each level building upon the previous one. Yet no layer determines subsequent ones, so that the final shape of women's informal associations cannot be predicted until all the elements contributing to their collective legitimacy have been interlocked.

Somewhere at the heart of women's informal associations lies kinship. Birth into a family group defines a set of kin relations which in turn define the most elemental structures of the women's subsociety.

---

[4]The legitimacy of women's power base is, of course, separate from the ramifying legitimacy that is accorded to women's power in general. By admitting to the variability of the size of any given 'public,' we have plainly left open this second question of whether women's power, exercised largely through informal associations, achieves substantial recognition throughout a society. Collective acceptance of an association by its constituents may not correspond to a society-wide acknowledgment of women's power as exercised through that association. But this says more about inconsistencies in ideology from one societal level to another than it tells about the illegitimate exercise of power by informal associations.

Birth is far from a natural event; the social and cultural ties surrounding birth give newborns a social identity within a set of allied kin and confer specific rights, obligations, and resources. Women, like men, are born into families and kin groups, but the associations that they traditionally form both in and in-between those groups are often less well understood by social analysts. Even though these kin-based associations among women constitute the structural core of women's worlds in most cultures, they have remained submerged, subordinated both by the terms of descriptions or analysis (ethnographic or sexist bias) and by the power relationships in the formal society itself (sexual stratification).

Matriliny

The public legitimacy of women's solidarity is often assumed to be greatest where formal descent is traced through women, mother to daughter in a matriline. Matriliny places groups of mothers and sisters at the conceptual core of kin-based associations so that relationships traced through women are central to one's social self-definition. Although it is clear that women have considerable power and authority in systems where descent group membership is traced through their mothers, matriliny does not create female oligarchies (Douglas 1971). New studies of important historical matrilinies, like the Iroquois, show that the relative social, political, and economic powers of women and men were carefully counterpoised in a complex system of checks and balances (Brown 1975; Hewitt 1932; Randle 1951; Richards 1957; Wallace 1971). Studies of contemporary matriliny show a similar complexity (Krige and Krige 1943; Loeb 1934; Schlegel 1972; Schneider and Gough 1961). In all these cases, although men as fathers and husbands have limited roles, mothers and daughters share important resources and decision-making rights with brothers, sons and maternal uncles.

Patriliny

Women's rights in patrilineages are often misunderstood and even ignored. The claims women can press upon their natal patrilineages are rarely identical to men's, and they are sometimes not as explicitly recognized as men's. But women in nearly all such systems continue to have clearly definable relations with their natal kin.

In some societies, like the Sherpa or Tamang of Nepal (March 1979), even though descent is traced only through men, patrilineally related sisters remain important to one another and to their brothers all their lives. The Tamang explicitly recognize these ties: a woman calls her patrilineal clanswomen anonyinchon, while a man calls his busing. Toward anonyinchon and busing, women and men have definite social and ritual obligations with both political and economic implications.

In some African communities, patrilineally related women are organized into named informal associations. Green (1964), Okonjo (1976), and Van Allen (1976) all discuss the otu umuada, 'daughters of the lineage,' in West Africa:

The otu umuada included all the married, unmarried, widowed, and divorced daughters of a lineage or village group. These women acted as political pressure groups in their natal villages in order to achieve desired objectives. They stopped quarrels and prevented wars. So powerful was their reputation that their natal villages had to reckon with them and their possible reaction to every major decision (Okonjo 1976: 52).

These patrilineally related women were systematically organized into informal associations that gave them explicit rights and obligations throughout their lives in the lineages and communities of their birth.

In other cases, as in the traditional Taiwan described by M. Wolf √ (1972), the rights and duties of patrilineal sisters and daughters are highly circumscribed. In such societies, men do indeed comprise not only the conceptual, but the functional, core of patrilineal groups. Daughters can be nearly forgotten when they marry; sisters' and brothers' interests in one another are limited to relatively few ritual occasions.

It is not, then, that women around the world have no rights in their √ natal patrilineages, but rather that there is a wide range in those rights. The extent to which women, as sisters and daughters, continue to be reckoned in the logic of patriliny is much more highly variable than the intrinsic inclusion of brothers and sons in matriliny.

Bilaterality

In many parts of the world, one's kin group and sense of family extends to individuals on both the mother's and the father's side. Such bilateral systems offer considerable scope for women's kin-based informal associations.

Kinship ties in bilateral kindreds are activated by personal effort. Although kin are defined by birth, specific relatives become important as constituent allies only if relations with them are cultivated and maintained. This can result in a kind of 'playing off' of one side of the family, or set of kin, against another, as individuals vie for constituencies and patrons. Because inheritance and residence patterns may give women and men substantially different rights and resources, their respective strategies for alliance building can be very different. These differences profoundly shape women's personal networks and informal associations based on bilateral kinship.

ALLIANCES AFTER MARRIAGE

As a woman matures, new personages move into her original circle of kin. Marriage patterns often require that a woman move to live in a new household or community, but traditions may demand either that she sever old ties with her natal kin and community, or that she carefully maintain them as part of her legitimating constituency throughout her life.

Ties to Natal Home

In parts of Africa, women in the named associations of patrilineal 'daughters of the village' (otu umuada, see earlier discussion) live in the villages of their husbands, but as 'daughters' [sisters and paternal aunts] they are responsible for specific rites and sacrifices performed for the benefit of their patrilineal ancestors. They are (or were) also important in the resolution of certain types of disputes, especially accusations of adultery, inside their natal villages; moreover, they played pivotal roles mediating disputes between villages as well. Because the married women in the umuada tended to be dispersed in the different communities of their husbands, the meetings of the association of umuada daughters were held in rotation — moving from the marital community of one (patrilineally related, but virilocally married) woman to another. In this way, the associations "formed an important part of the communication network" in the entire society (Van Allen 1976: 68).

In many societies, the associations of related women dispersed by marriage are not so highly organized; similar principles, however, continue to apply. Throughout the rest of the world, in Southeast Asia and Oceania (M. Strathern 1972), Latin America (Isbell 1977), South Asia (Jacobson 1974; March 1979), and the Middle East (Mahsen 1969), examples abound of daughters' continued commitment to their natal group or village. In many or all of these examples, the demeanor of a village 'daughter' while living or visiting in her natal home is relatively unrestrained; it stands in sharp contrast to the behavior commonly expected of them as 'wives' in their husbands' homes or communities, where they must be respectful and reserved while conscientious and hard-working (see especially Berreman 1972). Under such circumstances, it would be reasonable to assume that women acting as 'daughters' are far more likely to be able to institute changes, press demands, or mobilize male support than they are in their more constrained roles as 'wives,' since their public legitimacy as daughters is more widely based in the lineage community than that of a wife in her marital domestic home.

Ties in Marital Community

A woman may eventually establish strong bonds of solidarity with the women of her marital household, hamlet or village, thereby expanding her constituent basis for legitimate action. Living in close proximity and sharing a lifestyle may foster mutual identification and friendship among women. In other instances, proximity is reinforced by working together. Women who share specific tasks, whether as domestic responsibilities or occupational opportunities, may themselves develop into a legitimate constituency of mutual support.

Like the legitimacy of women's associations resulting from other bases, constituencies sanctioning these associations, too, vary considerably. Some arise in reaction to women's relatively greater isolation from lineal kin groups after marriage, as in the case of traditional Taiwan (M. Wolf 1972). Others emerge even though women continue to be involved in their natal kin groups (March 1979; Strathern 1972). In all cases, however, important bases for establishing informal associations among women lie in their residential proximity after marriage and the labors they share as adult married women. Women, as wives and mothers, establish close ties with other wives and mothers who live and work with or near them.

In some instances, the creation of a solidary women's constituency is facilitated by neighborhood architecture, as when houses open onto a common court, share a common water fountain, or are clustered in some other way which encourages regular intimate contact between in-married women from different households. Cornelisen describes the lively existence of women on the adjoining back porches in their slum dwellings in Sicily (1977). Cronin points out that these contacts encourage women to develop important street networks, which teach concrete techniques for influencing decisions and controlling others. Friendship is not a positive cultural value in Sicily, but the street is nonetheless the "living room of all working-class families" (Cronin 1977:77). Among the women, young girls are included in the discussions that take place; and older women take frequent opportunities to teach them strategies, especially about dealing with men.

Even where the design and placement of houses do not themselves promote easy informal interaction among women, neighborhood associations may flourish because of women's shared or similar activites. Where the sexual division of labor has not privatized women's domestic labor, it places women in constant collaboration in the daily tasks of their houses. We will discuss the implications of the sexual division of labor in the following sections about the importance of explicitly economic informal associations, and here only note that women around the world commonly gather in the course of their everyday work and that this is often sufficient basis for solidarity and legitimacy. Hauling water, gathering fodder, washing clothes, and even preparing the family meals often put women into cooperative contact and predispose them to support one another.

Women's residential and occupational solidarity is extremely common worldwide, but it is at times noticeably constrained when obligations of work and residence are at odds. Even though women's domestic work may be identical, to the extent that their similar tasks are privatized into isolated domiciles, no work-based solidarity may be generated among them. To the extent, too, that husbands, sons, lovers, and fathers-in-law are important to women, men may be drawn into women's networks. Men may bring new resources and opportunities into women's lives, but at the same time, women's primary identification with their men's interests can undermine the collective sanctions of female solidarity across households.

Visiting, Gossiping, and Community Politics

In many communities, women maintain many of the interfamily village commitments, such as sick visits or condolence calls. Especially as women get older and become more established members of their marital communities, the reasons for their mutual visiting become increasingly diffuse. Even in South Asia, where the movements of recent brides are sharply restricted, older women "can always find a few others ready to sit down with them especially in the middle of the day, for a bit of gossip. And even the [daughters-in-law]in the house where the older women gather, have the pleasure of listening, though they do not speak" (Wiser and Wiser 1965: 147). The casual visiting and conversation among women who become friends in their marital villages provide not only, as we have said, support and companionship for vulnerable women, but also constitute the basis from which women begin to acquire collective sanctions for real active power and hence a legitimate constituency within the communities of their husbands.

Cross-culturally, gossip is a key weapon in the arsenal of otherwise unrelated women married into their husbands' communities. It is, as Harding's excellent study of gossip indicates, "potentially a challenge to the male hierarchy, a challenge to men's control of hierarchy. It is the politics of the officially powerless" (1975: 303). M. Wolf (1972) indicates that, even among the strongly patriarchal families and communities found in rural Taiwan, neighborhood associations of women are powerful brokers of public opinion. In a culture where individuals must preserve 'face,' words circulated among women have devastating potential. Lomnitz (n.d.) has made similar observations in a working-class district in Mexico. From their association with an older woman in the neighborhood, wives with drunken or unruly husbands received ample encouragement to challenge the men openly. Women's gossip, ridicule and bawdy humor can make and break reputations; men in many places justifiably regard these sessions with unease.

But gossip is not only about people; it communicates information about both tradition and change. It is a uniquely powerful form of communication since it not only transmits ideas, but also consolidates opinions about those ideas. "Gossip," says Harding, "is a system for circulating real information, but that is never all that is circulated. Although overt criticism is rare, covert evaluation is constant. The evaluation is conveyed by editing if not by editorializing" (1975: 301). Residentially and occupationally allied women do not only share information. Collectively they use information and their informal associations to wield considerable power.

In the African instances mentioned earlier in this chapter, the kinship-based association of the 'daughters of the village' is paralleled by another equally important association, the 'wives of the village' (Okonjo 1976; Van Allen 1976). Just as the 'daughters of the village' was a ritually and politically powerful association of women born to localized patrilineages, so, analogously, 'the wives of the village' was a similar association consisting of all the women who had married into a particular village. Even though these women were originally from various other villages and lineages, as 'wives,' they shared many interests. Every woman in these African societies, of course, belonged to both kinds of associations: as a daughter of one lineage and village, she shared concerns and was solidary with other daughters; as a wife married into another village and lineage, she united with other wives in the same position.

'Wives of the village' were the core organizers of <u>mikiri</u>, "the gatherings which performed the major role in self-rule among women and which articulated women's interests <u>as opposed to</u> those of men" (Van Allen 1976: 168, emphasis in the original). Mikiri gatherings could be called anytime to discuss and deliberate action on women's issues (Green (1947) 1964: 178-216). Debates were lively and open to all women, providing an animated forum in which many women acquired or exercised oratory and leadership skills (Van Allen 1972: 168). The mikiri meetings were particularly important in regulating women's trading and the markets by establishing dates, prices, market rituals, and other rules regarding the markets. But the authority and power of the mikiri extended into many other areas of West African life as well: thus, a man's mistreatment of his wife, failure to keep livestock out of women's fields, rowdy behavior in the markets, or sexual insults directed at women could all motivate mikiri inter-vention (Green (1947) 1964: 180; Leith-Ross 1939: 106-107; Van Allen 1972: 167- 168).

The communal sanctions available to women in enforcing their mikiri decisions were powerful. Beyond requests and persuasion, the women could engage in boycotts, strikes, levy fines, and even join in a unique form of reprisal called 'sitting on a man,' (see Chapter 5) in which an offender, usually male, would be identified, humiliated, and punished by a raucous and rampaging horde of women (Green (1947) 1964: 196-197; Harris 1940: 146-148; Leith-Ross 1939: 109; Van Allen 1979: 168-170). In short, the political, economic, and personal support these in-married wives could give one another was so substantial that it could override the expressed interests of their men.

SOLIDARITY, LEGITIMACY, AND POWER

Residence and women's patterns of work, then, together with kinship, do not simply confine or define women. They represent the most fundamental bases for association and shared world views among women, and are often widely accepted among the men and women of a society as principles for association. Sanctioned by so broad a constituency, women's associations based on these fundamental principles often gain a wide berth for political action.

These sources of solidarity, however, give rise to associations of greatly varied structure, purpose and impact. Each of them is only imperfectly separable from all the other bases. Birth into a particular kind of kin group, life in any of the many types of households and communities, and the many patterns of work and wider alliance must be considered simultaneously in order to understand the bases for constituting the informal associations of any given women's subsociety. In some circumstances, alliances based on one aspect, such as matrilineal kinship, may be reinforced by a daughter's continuing residence with her mother or by patterns of mother-daughter occupational cooperation. In other instances, the various bases compete with and undermine one another because of the different principles each embodies: one can readily document, for example, societies in which kinship is traced through men, where most nuclear families reside independently, but where wives from separate households and lineages cooperate extensively in their daily labors.

Each basis for association constitutes a separate thread in the overall web of female solidarity. Although each base can be found in one form or another, shaping the worlds of women everywhere, nowhere will the exact total configuration be identical. What is highlighted in one culture may be almost completely submerged in another; relations that are explicitly and outspokenly recognized as a source of solidarity in one situation will go carefully unspoken in another. The extent to which men are active in women's networks and associations also differs dramatically across cultures; similarly, the degree to which women's informal associations are able to cross-cut class and other social divisions is extremely variable.

If no blueprint can emerge, and each historical case requires its own specific analysis, it is nevertheless possible to frame an initial approach to women's informal associations. To determine the effectiveness of the association as a basis for social and political power, it is essential to explore the several bases of association and solidarity; to consider how strong these ties remain or become over a woman's life span; to evaluate how widely the collective sanction of these bases legitimates women's informal associations; to explore the full balance of rights, resources, and obligations conferred by these associations; and to determine where, as a result, the relative strengths of men and women lie.

SHAHSEVAN: AN INTRODUCTION TO THE WOMEN'S WORLD

As an illustration, it is useful to consider one concrete example more fully. Tapper's study (1978) of women's feasting networks among the Shahsevan semi-nomads of northeast Azerbaijan, Iran, presents a good case. It describes informal associations that permeate the domestic realm, but nonetheless extend women's influence into both a public world of their own as well as into the one that they share with the men. Tapper shows how intricately structured these associations are, how crucial they become in the political, economic, social, and religious life of their communities, and how they are tied to the more formal men's world. And, to explain their influence, Tapper analyzes the public sanction that legitimates them.

Among the Shahsevan, two main sources structure the women's informal world. First, informal associations take shape around the mundane daily connections between women within the domestic household and nomadic camp. The core residential as well as political group among the Shahsevan is defined by the seasonal fragmentation and reassemblage of segmentary patrilineages. Women marry into the patrigroups of their husbands. During the summer months, smaller herding clusters consist of about five tents, each containing a single domestic household of about seven or eight individuals -- ideally a senior man and wife, their unmarried children, married sons and wives, and sons' children. In winter, however, these settlements gather together so that there may be as many as fifteen such domestic tents living in a single camp.

The formal leadership of these camps is strictly "held to be a male prerogative" (Tapper 1978: 377). Senior men in camps, called aq saqal (literally 'grey beard' and formerly actually older men, but today increasingly politically assertive younger men as well), resolve public disputes and make major economic decisions, many of which center on herding and pasturage concerns. In the daily life of these camps, women acquire most of their initial position with reference to men. An adult woman's social, political, economic, and religious starting point rests in the position and status of her husband.

But to acquire the fullest authority and power among other women and in the community at large, derived status is not enough. To reach the pinnacles of power open to women in Shahsevan society a woman must either build upon these initially prestigious positions through actions of her own, or she must forge a position based entirely on her own achievements. Women achieve independent status in three main spheres: the religious, the domestic, and the magico-medical. Women who are returned pilgrims or ceremonial cooks become the core figures of influence, power, and authority among Shahsevan women; they come to be called aq birchek (literally 'grey hairs' or, as the men sometimes put it, a "women's aq saqal") (Tapper 1978: 384) in their own right. Women who acquire skill and renown as midwives are also accorded considerable respect.

All three hold positions of striking privilege. They are likely to attend as many as three times the feasts attended by average women, thus not only enjoying greater opportunities for sociality, but also greater access to community opinion and input into its formation. In daily life, too, they can expect help in domestic labors from a wider circle of women without having to reciprocate. They are the central nodes in women's authority, communication, and opinion networks. They are also the central nodes in connecting the women's networks to men. Women leaders transcend usual rules regarding female modesty and interact directly with influential men in their camps and communities. They can move about relatively freely, and converse with men openly, expressing "unsolicited opinions on numerous topics", in a more or less equal fashion to the male leaders (Tapper 1978: 388).

The second source of structure to women's informal associations, and the domain in which there is the greatest play for women's authority, lies in the networks of reciprocal relationships established through feasting exchanges. These relations and the network they create are called kheyr-u-sharr. Although the rules for establishing kheyr-u-sharr are the same for men and women, no two people's kheyr-u-sharr networks are exactly the same because each kheyr-u-sharr is an entirely egocentric network reflecting the relative power and influence of the particular person in question. Husbands and wives do not even have the same kheyr-u-sharr networks.

The most dramatic enactment of kheyr-u-sharr relations occurs at feasts. Feasts are the entertainment high point and center stage for playing out these all important relationships in Shahsevan society. They crystallize around the main life-cycle events of circumcision, betrothal, marriage, and death. Both women and men attend, but because they gather in separate tents and take part in separate feasting networks, the structure of authority relations for men and women are separate, though not unconnected. In their separate tents, seats of honor are reserved among men especially for aq saqal (male political leaders) and returned pilgrims and, similarly, among women for aq birchek (female political leaders), returned pilgrims and the wives of the male leaders and pilgrims.

For the women in particular, feasts are their main, if not their only, source of contact outside the domestic household and camp circle of kin. Conversations result in the exchange of vital information concerning marriage possibilities for children, markets and the sale of animals, recent pilgrimages, and the availability and quality of pasturage in other areas. All of this information is important to women and their families since it provides an alternate channel for verifying information that is vital to the well-being of the household and camp. In the general airing before the assembled guests, community disputes are heard and mediated; similarly, community decisions result from the opinions presented at feasts. In all these aspects, women's participation in feasts is very like men's. Both attend because of their places in kheyr-u-sharr networks, each socializes separately, and each uses the occasion to glean information from sources outside their own camp and participate in wider political displays, decision-making and dispute-settlement.

But the structure of women's activities at feasts differs in one important respect: the cooking tent. During the course of a feast, apart from the general assembly of ranked guests, an influential knot of women gathers in the cooking tent. This inner circle consists of the most powerful women: the ceremonial cook herself, aq birchek, and pilgrims. Some of these women might also be wives of prominent men, but their place in this inner circle depends upon their own successes as leaders, not their husbands'. In the cooking tent, these women leaders exchange important information and arbitrate major disputes not in the formal way of guests in the main tents, but in an open atmosphere of equality and mutual respect. Moreover, the place each of the female notables in the cook tent holds in the daily life of her local community means that announcements, arbitration, and advice settled upon in the cook tent find their way back into communities throughout Shahsevan society:

> It is interesting to note that the comparatively rigid seating arrangements of the guest tent are determined largely by factors of ascribed status, while personal factors and achieved status tend to disrupt any such formal ranking system. This is demonstrated when the notables following the ceremonial cook into the kitchen tent make no effort to order their places there. The equality pervading relations in the kitchen tent is striking; indeed, each women represents a combination of achieved and ascribed status that renders her a leader in her own right. An aq birchek leads the discussion of controversial subjects, but in this select group she is no more than prima inter pares.

> Major quarrels are aired and to some extent arbitrated by the women in the kitchen tent at each feast. Decisions reached here can with some ease be relayed to both those women not present in the kitchen tent and those who have not attended the feast at all (Tapper 1980 (1978): 391).

In all these ways, then, Tapper claims that the informal kheyr-u-sharr relationships and networks are central to the structure of what she calls the "women's subsociety" among the Shahsevan. It is a 'sub' society because it is partially derived from male-defined statuses, and because of the primacy accorded to men and male leadership in formal spheres. From this perspective, the women's exchanges are complementary and subordinate. From another perspective, the women's exchanges ultimately constitute something of an independent 'society,' structured around women's own kheyr-u-sharr and achieved statuses. "The ideology of kheyr-u-sharr is the basis of a network; every woman is linked with other women, each of whom has kheyr-u-sharr ties with yet others. This network is bounded only by the fact that it is exclusive to women" (Tapper 1978: 393-394). Within the informal associations established in the overlapping circles of women's kheyr-u-sharr and the informal connections women have within their own tents and camps, the structure of women's leadership and communication networks among the Shahsevan emerges.

In this case, women's leadership and communication systems are crucial to the perpetuation of tradition. Because the men's and women's sex-specific kheyr-u-sharr networks are based on publicly sanctioned criteria for association, they attain community-wide legitimacy and generate separate structures of authority. The women's networks can, therefore, constitute an independent collective voice for women's opinion. Moreover, because the women's leaders are allowed to express those opinions in front of men outside of feast contexts, their advice and the women's point of view has a strong foothold, albeit informal, in the formal world of men. Often the women's leaders, particularly the pilgrims, are relatively conservative so that they tend to consolidate, disseminate, and garner community support for "a pool of traditional ideas and concepts of correct behavior" (Tapper 1978: 393). As individuals of some experience and with exceptional access to community opinion, they are very well informed and "their advice is a valuable guide to acceptable behavior" (Tapper 1978: 387 emphasis in original).

Feminine authority among the Shahsevan, however, is not closed to change. In one instance reported by Tapper, the women's subsociety, presumably with the sponsorship and guidance of the women's leaders, learned about the connection between cancer and smoking, and exerted considerable pressure to reduce cigarette consumption. "This preoccupation not only had noticeable effects on the women's smoking habits, but on the men's as well, since many women keep the keys to the trunks where their husband's cigarette supplies are stored" (Tapper 1978: 395).

PART TWO

Dynamics of the Informal Sphere

3

Informal Associations:
Defensive or Active?

ACTIVE AND REACTIVE STRATEGIES

The Shahsevan example points to a fundamental tension between the active and reactive qualities of informal associations. Once preconceptions about the discreteness of the private domain are set aside, the automatic depiction of women's informal associations as passive, supportive, domestic, disorganized, and apolitical also vanishes. It becomes possible to recognize women as active social and political individuals who consolidate their autonomy through informal alliances. Even within this perspective, though, it is also plain that women's informal associations sometimes coalesce as defensive responses to crises or constraints beyond women's control. For all their resourcefulness, such defensive associations can do little to combat the constraints that shape them. Characterization of women's associations as active or reactive does not necessarily reflect observer bias, but acknowledges these countervailing tendencies.

As Bujra points out in the introduction to a collection of studies on women's solidarity: "It is important . . . to ask ourselves whether the 'solidarity' exhibited by women in these various situations is merely a 'forced solidarity' based solely on women's mutual exclusion from male society, in other words, sexual segregation" (1979: 31) or whether the women's associations are capable of "pursuing a more active unity" (1979: 16). Because the ethnographic record often describes weaknesses in women's social position — such as the fragility of marriage or the unreliability of husbands -- or in their economic position, women's attempts to protect themselves and, typically, their children can often be seen as defensive responses. They are a kind of cooperation necessitated by shared adversity. In direct contrast, other mutual support systems not only provide emergency or auxiliary protection but may establish resources of their own to create real alternatives for women. "In this sense female solidarity is more clearly an 'offensive' activity, designed to provide female alternatives to dependence on male breadwinners" (Bujra 1979: 30).

The extent to which an informal association uses defensive or active strategies determines the degree to which it can be receptive to development interventions. Although no informal association is exclusively defensive or active, some are better able to undertake specific initiatives. Their objectives are more explicit and their organization and resource capabilities are more nearly consonant with those objectives. It is with associations of this sort, we shall show, that the development effort can begin.

On the other hand, the strategies that we call 'defensive' represent the efforts of politically disenfranchised groups of people with insufficient resources to meet even their most minimal needs. The organizational styles of these groups are interesting because they structure leadership, responsibility, and participation to redistribute insufficient resources and meet the emergency needs of members, if only temporarily and serially. They create important patterns of communication and exchange and thus afford essential insights into a community's internal dynamics. Although these associations serve women primarily, they also work on behalf of a wider constituency that includes children, kinfolk, or neighbors. In many places, women's defensive associations provide the most effective — if not the only — indemnity against scarcity and constant crisis.

These defensive associations, though, remain permanently inaccessible as vehicles of development. To intervene or not to intervene in these cases is not just a question of ethics but of practicality: defensive informal associations are so transformed by any outside intervention that they cease to be the kind of association that the intervention wanted to reach. The original association will, with luck, take its creativity, resourcefulness, flexibility, and retreat before intervention advances, to regroup sub rosa once more. The poorest of the world's poor cannot sustain such well-intentioned but ill-conceived assaults on their meager defenses.

In planning for development, then, we must distinguish between the defensive strategies of some informal associations as opposed to more active strategies. While the defensive ones must basically be left alone lest we further endanger them, they remain important channels for communication and sources of insight for outside observers.

THE 'WOMAN NETWORK' AS A DEFENSIVE STRATEGY

Informal associations can be characterized as defensive when they mobilize in response to adversity or crisis. These are basically reactive social relationships that do not aim to create separate resources, alternative conditions, or autonomous influence. They are based not just on women's mutual exclusion from male society, in Bujra's phrase, but also on other shared deprivations.

Women's ties, as we have seen, are bound by the imperatives of family, community, and work. But, whether they are embedded in kinship ties, or extend effectively to unrelated friends and neighbors, even defensive networks are outside of, and complementary to, marriage and the nuclear household. They can, moreover, be reinforced by a shared identity as women. Even where women's networks are internally stratified, for example, a prevailing idiom of equality among women often masks differences in riches and influence. The overall ethic generated by these converging pressures and shared burdens is one of mutual aid, according to which, in the words of the Kenyan women described by Nelson, "women must help each other" (1979).

Women rally behind one another to meet a host of difficulties. They come to each other's rescue many times a day, for reasons which will undoubtedly ring resoundingly familiar to any woman anywhere who has ever been pressed by daily events. Children wander off, become unruly, or simply demand attention when a woman is engaged in other tasks;

dinner boils over, isn't cooked, or lacks salt (sugar, butter, spice . . .); husbands, lovers, or customers run off (get drunk, angry, unreasonable . . .); an errand must be run, a bill paid, an alibi provided, bail raised, cows milked, firewood or water hauled, clothes washed or mended. In all the myriad tasks for which women are responsible, in all the multiple relations women sustain, women must know someone who will occasionally relieve them. Because women's daily support needs cannot be easily predicted in advance, it is difficult to prearrange aid on a contractual basis. Because they frequently involve jobs that are themselves personally unrewarding, physically unpleasant, and largely unvalued by wider male society, only a strong interpersonal ethic of mutual obligation can motivate assistance.

Caring for children is one of the most common tasks assigned to women by the sexual division of labor. The demands of child care often motivate a woman to turn to her friends and relations for help. Women look not only to their own mothers, daughters or extended families for assistance, but also to friends and neighbors — to whom they sometimes give fictive kinship titles. Shantytown mothers may leave their children with a neighborhood 'aunt' or 'grandmother'; in many villages, small children spend a great deal of time with elder sisters, extended family members, or sometimes their mothers' cowives. Such practices are a regular feature of life in many settings where women are heads of households or are economically active outside their homes; they have been described even in contemporary Western situations (Bott 1957; Stack 1974).

Many of these ties have remained poorly defined in existing analyses because they appear, from the vantage of western cultural and historical experience, to be rooted not in social relations with political and economic consequences, but instead in relations of purely 'natural' origins. Mothering is, however, a cultural act. It is not simply that women as mothers must, or must want to, fulfill their children's needs. Their fates are tied to their children not by the biological imperatives of motherhood, but by the pursuit of political, social, or economic opportunity and security. Maternal devotion is integral to the personal strategies of women and gives meaning to their actions.

The structural core of these associations is what M. Wolf has called the 'uterine family': a mother and her children (1972: 32-37). This social reproductive unit is deceptively simple: it actually gives rise to many complex economic and political relationships of great importance to women. "The uterine family has no ideology, no formal structure, and no public existence. It is built out of sentiments and loyalties that die with its members, but it is no less real for all that" (M. Wolf 1972: 37). Even in the absence of culturally recognized descent from the mother or lifelong residence with her, motherhood commonly creates vital ties with children.

A variety of different pressures reinforce the solidarity of mothers and children or cause it to take somewhat different shapes. Sex segregation resulting in women's exclusion from public activity may, as L. Fallers and M. Fallers have reported in Turkey (1976), greatly reinforce women's bonds to mothers, daughters and sisters in spite of the formal priority of male-defined ties. Different patterns of inheritance can emphasize mother-daughter, sister-sister, or sister-brother ties. Similarly, different ritual obligations such as puberty rites or ancestral worship within the natal group can create special additional ties between mothers and daughters, sisters, or sisters and brothers.

In the absence of formal or public avenues to political authority, mothers frequently manipulate children as political pawns. In circumstances where women are almost completely disenfranchised from official authority, such as in the traditional Taiwanese case described by M. Wolf, a mother constructs deep personal and psychological bonds with children both by her own 'selfless' devotion and by keeping their relationship with their father formal and disciplinarian (1972: 160-161). Mothers not only undertake the laborious personal care of children and identify with them, but also frequently commit many of their own resources for their children's advancement. In many parts of the world, mothers assume the burden of financing children's educations, even to the point of investing their own retirement funds to enhance their children's career opportunities (Fernea 1969; Mintz 1971).

Women cast their fates with their children in other ways as well. Many of the most important informal associations and alliances established by women are forged in the names of their children and their children's needs. Fosterage, child-swapping, and ritual co-parentage create strong bonds of mutual obligation which have far-reaching effects on the economic, political, and social opportunities of parents as well as children. In her excellent study, Stack has shown how ties created through children provide the basic channel for the circulation of critical resources among poor urban blacks in the U.S. (1974). Dubisch has reviewed the literature on the circum-Mediterranean — Southern Europe, the Middle East, and North Africa — to show that mutual child-sharing is one of the central activities cementing mother-daughter and sister-sister ties, regardless of other rules of descent or residence (1977).

These studies underscore a crucial point: that the ties mothers create through children are able to motivate sharing and mutual support among the chronically poor. The associations women form around children are so intensely personal and informally flexible that they compel exchange and make mutual assistance possible. Even though need necessarily outstrips resources among the poor, mutual assistance can, at least temporarily, stave off disaster. Ties through children create an idiom of extremely powerful obligation — to nurture and support unstintingly. The unique emotional strength of such bonds makes them capable of surviving in times of stress and under difficult circumstances when few other kinds of ties can.

In caring for the general domestic needs of their households, women also turn to one another. Scarcity, and not simply the sexual division of labor, often throws them into mutual interdependence. Whether sharing a neighborhood oven or pooling their labor, women often evolve cooperative arrangements for performing many household tasks. Extensive networks of borrowing and lending frequently complement the exchanges of labor, allowing women some flexibility in their disposal of limited resources such as money, food, and household goods.

Women's exchanges of goods occur on a mundane level in everyday household and community life, but they become acutely important in times of economic stress. Among the Sherpa and Tamang of highland Nepal, for example, although sons (and not daughters) inherit land from their parents, daughters retain certain rights in their parental household after they have moved to their husbands' villages. Even after her parents are dead, a married woman may return to her natal village to obtain money, food, or other kinds of assistance from her brothers living in the ancestral home. She might also turn to her sisters, living in the villages of their husbands. The obligations of brothers and sisters constitute, through the women who have married into different houses and/or localities, a web of security against localized crop failure, sudden severe illness or other domestic economic crisis. The importance of ties traced through women as a kind of insurance against local crisis has been reported for many (even most) other parts of the world — in South Asia, Oceania, Latin America, the Middle East, and parts of Africa. Even in the U.S., where access to economic resources is highly rationalized, Bott reports that women turn to networks of "maternal kin as an informal insurance policy" (1957:138).

Thus, women turn to each other not only in times of daily crisis, but in the sporadic times of serious personal or familial difficulty. Some of these crises arise at major turning points in women's life cycles. Marriage and dislocation into another household or community present many women with their first real need for female solidarity and support. Sherpa women in Nepal, for example, are extremely reluctant to marry into a village where no other woman from their home community yet lives: who, they ask, would tell them which people to trust, whom to avoid, where to find water, wood, grazing lands; who, in short, would help them readapt to their new home? (March 1979). In some instances, women inside a bride's marital home will come to help her. Nepalese Tamang women, who frequently marry their mothers' brothers' sons or their fathers' sisters' sons, have a kinswoman, their 'aunt,' for a co-resident mother-in-law (March 1979).

Women in other parts of the world, not blessed with benevolent mothers-in-law, may have to turn outside the household for their first allies. Thus, describing the bride's adjustment in rural Taiwan, M. Wolf indicates: "Once a young bride has established herself as a member of the women's community, she has also established for herself a certain amount of protection" (1972: 39). Wolf also described the plight of one young bride "who had little village backing in her troubles with her husband and his family as the result of her arrogance toward the women's community," (1972: 38-39), and another who married a shopkeeper's son and, "warned by her husband's parents not to be too 'easy' with the other villagers lest they try to buy things on credit...obeyed to the point of being considered unfriendly by the women of the village. When she began to have serious troubles with her husband and eventually his family, there was no one in the village she could turn to for solace, advice, and most important, peacemaking" (1972: 39).

Childbirth is another occasion in a woman's life cycle which typically leads her to draw on the assistance of other women. Several perceptions about childbirth blend to create a unique tableau of female solidarity and mutual support. First, of course, is the highly charged atmosphere of birth itself. The interdependence of women and children in the uterine family, as we have already discussed, makes the anticipation of a new infant doubly emotional. Expectant mothers, as well as the other women in the family, household or community, are aware of the importance of children to mothers, the status and esteem children bring mothers, and the ways in which new children can shift delicate balances and alliances among the adults around them. Although the anticipation is generally happy and the arrival of a new baby an occasion for joy, it is also an anxious time for women. Especially where medical care is lacking, intimate knowledge of maternal and infant suffering or death plunges many women into real fear. Even in the easiest of pregnancies and deliveries, women need support and relief. The tendency for women to turn to other experienced women in childbirth is accentuated because men in many parts of the world are strictly excluded and, even where they are allowed physically, codes of sexual modesty may cut a woman off from her husband emotionally in many ways.

In pregnancy and childbirth, women have devised countless ways, both physical and emotional, to help one another. Women may assist the new mother in locating and summoning the midwife, who is herself typically a woman. Sometimes the midwife begins caring for the expectant mother early in pregnancy, massaging and advising her (Paul 1974); sometimes she is not called until labor begins. Through the delivery, the midwife and other women counsel and console, sharing both medical and magical knowledge about birth. An important part of the support they give is emotional, trying to keep fearful sentiments away and encourage a more joyous interpretation of the event. Berger has written that the Middle Eastern belly dance originated as a ritual dance done by the circle of women attending a childbed (1961). A hard-working and quiet Tamang woman friend, whose two children had been born only after long and painful deliveries, described the gathering of friends and relations:

> When you go to have the baby — you have to have a friend. Sometimes it takes two days, sometimes three days. It's hard. When I had my second child, my son, it took two days. When I had my eldest daughter, it took three days....Everyone was there. Everyone came to see me. We sacrificed chickens for the ghosts and spirits. I don't remember any of it. All night long my mother held onto my hands, very tight. My mother-in-law held me. They held onto me all night (March: personal communication).

In addition, women commonly assume responsibility for the domestic work of the new mother, taking care of her other children and keeping her house running. In parts of traditional India, other women take over all her work, leaving the mother free to devote herself completely to the new infant for some time (Jacobson 1974: 110). Among the Tamang of north central Nepal, a lightened work load is the right of a new mother; it is the payment of her 'birth debt' (March, personal communication). Women friends and relations may also undertake whatever work is necessary to prepare a ritual feast to celebrate the child's birth or carry the tidings out to others in the mother's circle. Admiring and caring for the new baby may bring even rival women close. In Taiwan, where mothers and mothers-in-law are often locked in a bitter struggle for domestic supremacy, the younger woman's need for help smoothes out many tensions:

> In the first weeks after her child's birth, she turns repeatedly and gratefully to her mother-in-law for advice and assistance. Often the older women sleeps with her during the first few weeks in order to help her during the night and to make sure that the young father does not resume sexual relations with his wife too soon after childbirth. For both women this is a peaceful and happy time. The younger woman needs the advice and help, and the older woman is delighted to be intimately involved in her grandchild's care. In many families this period of shared concern sets a tone for the future

relations between the two women that prevents them from ever becoming serious enemies (M. Wolf 1972: 158).

Women also turn to one another at times of crisis in their children's lives. When a child is ill, it is women from the mother's support network who come to help with care of the other children, with family cooking, with locating a doctor, and even with raising the money for medical services. Alternatively, and perhaps even more commonly, other mothers advise on home remedies, spiritual causes of disease, and help each mother in her assessment of the nature and gravity of her own child's illness.

Not all her children's crises are unhappy, however; women are also essential to one another at the time of their children's marriages. When marriages are arranged, information gleaned from the mother's network of related and friendly women is usually decisive in the selection of spouses for both sons and daughters. Although the public negotiation of marriages is typically a male province, a multiplicity of women's gatherings and go-betweens have, as typically, already made the critical decisions. Even where marriages are not arranged for children, a mother relies on her support net to help prepare for and celebrate the marriage itself. Without the joint cooking and sewing endeavors of a woman's circle, marriages could not involve the elaborate displays or large communal festivities they often do. ,

Family catastrophes also activate women's networks. Serious prolonged illness and death are domestic crises for which few households are adequately prepared. Once again, it is the woman's circle of support which often undertakes the many tasks of consoling, visiting, and cooking for handicapped or bereaved families. If the wife is ill or dies, the women of her safety net may take over her domestic chores and childcare duties, even for extended periods of time, consoling the husband, and perhaps finding him a new wife. If the husband is incapacitated or dies, women rally around the overburdened woman with domestic help, and often are important in helping the woman cope with her widowhood. Frequently, women play prominent roles in funerary rites and mourning customs. Some women may become specialists in organizing large mortuary feasts.

Divorce and abandonment present other serious crises for women with children in most parts of the world. The husband's departure, or wife's rejection of the husband, forces a substantial realignment of allegiances and resources in which women rely most heavily on other women. The particular women to whom a divorced or abandoned woman turns will vary with the ethnographic circumstances. In situations where wives and children normally reside with their husband's extended families, a woman's ability to remain in that patrilocal household hinges upon her and her children's relations with her mother- and sisters-in-law far more than it depends upon relations with the men of that household.

If the rupture is complete, however, as it frequently is, women's networks become even more important. For women throughout the world, in a wide variety of kinship, marriage and residence systems, the tie to mother is the first line of defense against marital difficulties. As Dubisch (1977) has shown, throughout the Circum-Mediterranean regions women return, above all, to their mothers in times of marital crisis. Among uterine kin, and especially among mothers, daughters and sisters, the exchange of goods and services, such as reciprocal child care and fosterage, establishes a network of interdependent women. When any of their marriages fail, there is someone prepared to provide support and shelter through the crisis period. Similar patterns are repeated over much of the globe.

These defensive associations among women thus serve as an effective safety net for casualties of poverty, unemployment, abandonment, and illness. They represent a continuous and nearly universal mechanism for insulating households and even communities from disaster. The resources a women is able to control through her associations with other women not only protect her personally, but can shelter her children and often her entire marital household. Particularly in social settings where emergency is endemic and other channels of assistance are closed, then, the essential defenses that women's associations provide need to be recognized.

The capacity of defensive alliances to circulate resources also influences local economies. The compensatory qualities of women's networks should not be misinterpreted as passivity: taken together, the goods, services, information, and companionship that they exchange cannot be described as trivial. Nor should the orientation of defensive associations toward crisis suggest that they coalesce only haphazardly. On the contrary, support networks mobilize following culturally recognized cues.

Defensive associations among women, in other words, are so essential and ubiquitous as to merit greater recognition from planners; and they are so patterned and predictable as to permit systematic study. Ironically, though, the durability of these defensive alliances arises largely from women's vulnerability as a group. It is this paradox that makes them poor channels to outside agencies. Active intervention in women's protective associations will at best emphasize this vulnerability and, at worst, strip women's defenses away.

SOLIDARITY AS AN ACTIVE STRATEGY

A narrow focus on the defensive aspects of women's associations, masks their indirect impact on women's active solidarity. In reality, many of these associations often balance strategies along a narrow tightrope: at first glance they resemble the defensive attempts of vulnerable individuals to retain some modicum of control over their lives, but as one probes further they may begin to appear more confident and assertive as autonomous collectivities organized to manage resources and strategies.

Women who rally to one another at moments like childbirth, marriage or death are not just behaving as members of similar but separate family units: they are sharing an identity, and in the process they create an independent reference group, one that is, paradoxically, extra-domestic. Although this solidarity may indeed arise from weakness, it can become a political base, enhancing women's status and power vis-a-vis men. Alternatively, through their mutual help practices, women sometimes establish separate sources of material support, which may in turn blunt their vulnerability and dependence on men. As Yanagisako found in her study of the "female centrality" in Japanese immigrant networks in the U.S., "an individual's and a family's status in the community and their access to economic resources (such as jobs, capital and housing), leadership positions, and political alliances that translate into power are significantly affected by their position in these (women's) networks. A woman's informal solidary ties and her consequent ability to mobilize people, whether for holiday gatherings or for political action, are an important resource, both for herself and for the members of her family" (1977:222). Defensive strategies can, then, form the foundation for active political and economic behavior.

The extent to which women's informal associations legitimate an autonomous women's social reality and unite women in active solidarity varies considerably from culture to culture and from situation to situation. In some instances — such as the Moroccan case investigated by Maher — they may provide a safety net, but only improve women's status or bargaining position marginally. Elsewhere, and especially in some of the African examples of women's active resistance to men which we will examine, they help furnish women with an independent identity and serious powers of persuasion in their dealings with men. Even in settings of extreme sexual differentiation, women's associations promote confidence, organize leadership and resources, and thereby create leverage for women. Although the bases for an emergent active women's solidarity are quite diverse ethnographically, and although they may not invert the overall structural authority of men over women, they do redistribute power and resources in some very important ways.

Shared kinship and shared residence are two fundamental sources for active as well as defensive alliances among women. Beyond these basic social structures, moreover, there are a variety of other kinds of informal associations which must be considered. In particular, there are two additional bases from which collective action is commonly undertaken: they stem from women's shared labor obligations arising from sexual and domestic divisions of labor; and, they grow out of the female solidarity established in the fulfillment of women's ritual and religious obligations. These two additional sources for women's active solidarity are of special importance to us because it is within these domains that women acquire essential political skills and economic resources for change.

Even the most specialized of women's informal associations can serve wider personal and community needs, up to and including the most diffuse desire for companionship. But the more explicitly the purposes of any particular informal association are focused upon economic or political objectives within the community, the greater its potential role in planned change. Specifically, we want to look first at those informal associations which are more self-consciously economic in their purposes to see what kinds of resources women typically control, how they collectively or individually exercise that control, and particularly, how they redistribute the resources they control. In addition, we must examine how women fit into the structures of sociopolitical authority in their societies. We need to know what is the basis for women's authority within their communities and how they have organized themselves to activate or protect that authority. In many societies, for example, women derive much of their power and authority from religion and ritual. By studying the associations that grow out of either the economics of women's work or their religious and ritual activities we can understand the specific foundation of resources and authority on which to build change.

Women's labor and ritual obligations around the world have generated a wide variety of informal associations. These vary in scale, recruitment of members, structure of decision making, patterns for the distribution of resources, and embeddedness in wider social, economic, or political processes. They may be small, cooperative, open groups organized for the reciprocal exchange of labor or goods, such as neighborhood rotating labor or credit associations, or spontaneous prayer groups and feasting exchanges. But they can also range considerably larger and more complex, as in village-wide women's secret societies or multi-community road, trail, and irrigation-work projects. Even among more narrowly economic or political associations, there is wide variation. This variety has profound implications as we contemplate policy for intervention, since intervention often amplifies and reinforces existing relations. If we want, in our development plans, to enhance equal opportunity, not privilege, we must seek out women's informal associations that are not only economically or politically active, but are also structured on essentially egalitarian principles of membership and decision making, with a basically reciprocal and mutually supportive circulation of resources among that membership.

Many types of informal associations between women are used for the particular benefit of some women over others, or of some women's own families and social groups over others'. Such, for example, are the relationships between a domestic servant and her employer: in most cases such a relation is not strictly contractual but subsumes many complex mutual obligations; neither decision making nor the other benefits of the association, however, are evenly distributed between servant and mistress. Furthermore, as Stoler (1977) has shown, relations of patronage among women tend to undercut the bargaining power of the poor. In her study of class structure and female autonomy in a Javanese village, Stoler indicates that women from landless families typically find opportunities for wage labor by obligating themselves to a patron household. In this way, they can "earn the right" to harvest rice. But the "vertical, dyadic relationships" that emerge between landless and wealthier women, though of mutual benefit, "cross-cut the possible strength that women might gain by exerting collective pressure on a wealthy landowner" (Stoler 1977: 83). Women's options in this study were determined by their class position to an overwhelming degree, and women's associations simply perpetuated this reality (see also Burkett 1977).

Similarly, there are large-scale associations, such as women's church groups and auxiliaries, as well as many of those associations known in the literature as 'voluntary associations,' which, while also informal and active, ultimately promote the political and economic privileges of the advantaged few: households of village headmen or community leaders, wealthy lineages or 'first families,' specific ethnic or religious groups, and class-identified or elite groups are some examples (see also Taylor 1981). The claims of these other types of vested group interests may supersede female solidarity. As Bujra points out with regard to class-based versus female-based interests: "Female solidarity only overrides class divisions in very exceptional circumstances and it may indeed contribute to the perpetuation of those class divisions" (1979: 30).

It is important to distinguish among the active strategies of women's informal associations not only in terms of structural criteria such as scale, or functional criteria such as whether their efforts and/or resources are primarily economic or political, but also in terms of an overall judgment: is the association predominantly exploitative of some of its participants or does it attempt to support all mutually? The introduction of external resources or power into traditional systems, if they reach and affect the local system at all, can either reduce or exacerbate existing

differences of power, authority and wealth. Which of these two possibilities is realized depends upon the kinds of preexisting associations into
which the new resources and sources of power or authority are being
directed.

These questions cut through many of the complexities of women's
informal associations to highlight their potential role in development. We
have built upon these analytical distinctions to suggest a more pragmatic
methodology for assesing when intervention in women's informal associations can be appropriate. The tree diagram which follows "Identifying
Women's Informal Associations" (on page 46) not only summarizes the
questions raised thus far, but indicates also those which will be discussed
in the following two chapters on women's economic and ritual
associations. The crucial questions which must be asked about any
informal association, then, in order to assess its appropriateness for
intervention include, in sequence, those in Figure 1 (page 46).

4

Women's Economic Associations: Patterns in the Redistribution of Resources

ECONOMIC BASES FOR ORGANIZATION

Some of women's informal associations actively strengthen the economic position of women. Based upon the shared economics of being female, these associations are frequently the very networks through which women learn about work, find jobs, and accomplish their various tasks. Through their informal associations, women establish webs of economic support for themselves and their families, and ultimately forge alliances for both economic and political power in the community at large. With no outside intervention at all, these actively economic informal associations already mediate great changes for women; it is also in such associations that the greatest potential for planned change lies.

It is not surprising that associations with a clear economic orientation should figure so importantly among active informal associations. Mutual economic support is one obvious avenue to autonomy and control. Women find employment, for example, through their networks, especially casual jobs like hawking, housecleaning, or laundrywork, which are outside the formal economic sector and available primarily by way of contacts. In Mexico City, to cite but one example among many, Arizpe has noted that poor Indian migrant women are obliged to find work because most of the men in their midst work only occasionally and in poorly paid positions. Lacking other opportunities for jobs in the formal sector, the women usually turn to street selling, since the "network of former Mazahua migrants in the wholesale fruit and vegetable section of the Merced, the main city market, gives Mazahua women access to wholesale prices" (1977: 35).

The woman network described by Arizpe is both defensive and active at once. But, if the obstacles are not too great, women's shared economic strategies can demonstrably improve — and not just protect — women's position. The importance of women's network connections for locating significant economic opportunities, especially for women and their families who migrate into urban areas, has been stressed in numerous studies (see especially Gonzalez 1976; Kiray 1976 a & b; Little 1973; and Smith 1976). Some of these women's networks have been treated as a response to migration, but most have their roots in traditional relationships — kinship, regional or village ties, and patronage. Most revisionist views of rural-to-urban migration (Safa and du Toit 1973; Abu-Lughod 1961) have abandoned the once-prevailing emphasis on the disorganizing impact of the city on individuals and instead have discovered the importance of mutual bonds among migrants in easing the transition from village to town. The job of creating and sustaining social networks frequently falls to women. Men may have available the associations of the workplace and the coffee-house or tavern; but women

FIGURE 1

IDENTIFYING WOMEN'S INFORMAL ASSOCIATIONS

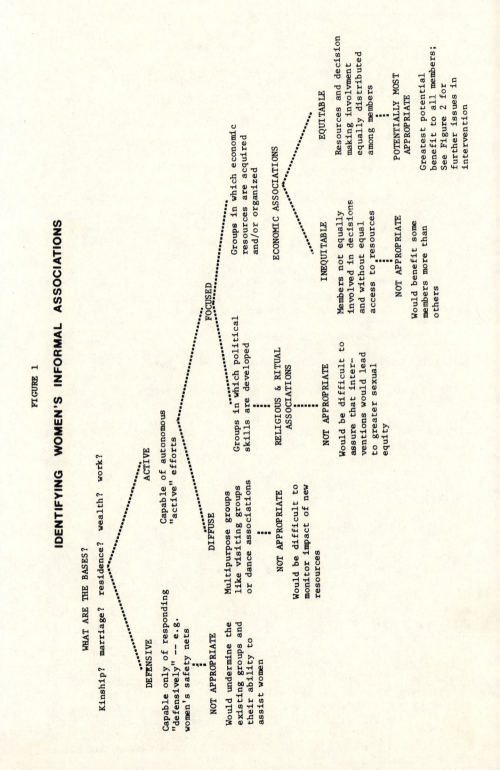

are able to establish a wide range of contacts as well as maintain old ones where their spouses cannot. It is ironic that it has taken so long for the central role played by women's informal associations in migration to gain explicit acknowledgment (Vatuk 1972).

These networks not only assist women economically, but often ✓ structure political patronage and/or solidarity for entire communities. Information about jobs and housing circulates rapidly among women, before as well as after migration. In some agrarian communities where women work closer to home than the men do, women may be the ones to glean outside information from pedlars and other itinerants (Riegelhaupt 1967; Cronin 1977). Ties within the woman network that bring migrant mothers back to their village homes to give birth or to find spouses for their children also serve as vital channels for news. The women of migrant and would-be migrant families thus become a valuable source of information.

In this way, new contacts are generated and new networks established. Domestic service in wealthy households can provide a particularly ✓ ✗ fruitful source of new connections and even some mobility (Riegelhaupt 1967). Maher has documented women's tenacity in cultivating patron- ✓ client ties with other women of higher social strata (1974). To sustain such a bond, a woman can call upon any number of strategies. She can, for example, make her employer a godmother or she can invite her to a wedding feast or birth celebration. Significantly, such manipulations can involve extensive exploitation of the 'bonds of womanhood' that transcend barriers of social class. An aspiring client can also perform an assortment of services beyond the domestic ones for which she was hired for her patron. In exchange, she wins the right to ask for favors and loans, gains access to other potential patrons and jobs, and with luck vouchsafes her own economic and social credit in the community. She may also learn her way around state institutions, since patrons teach by example and assistance, even to the extent of providing introductions to local officials.

Women who work in the same occupation or economic activity often cooperate to meet explicitly economic needs and in the process expand their effectiveness and influence. The women beer brewers of Kenya's Mathare Valley, for example, rely on network connections for "the buying and selling of buzaa [raw corn mash beer] wholesale and obtaining extended credit, exchanging information concerning the reliability of credit customers (male and female), putting up bail and collecting money for fines, and extended help in serious emergencies" (Nelson 1979: 86). These women have mobilized their dense personal networks to a series of strategic ends. Living in a squatter neighborhood, they are economically independent only because they manage to brew traditional beers, which are illegal in the urban area. In their short history in the area, they have formed a number of self-help groups to attain several goals that were important to them as women. Some contributed money and labor for the building of nursery schools; others campaigned to persuade the city council to put water pipes into the Valley. At various times the women sent delegations to influence politicians. Their occupational networks, then, engendered solidarity and gave them the capacity to establish short-term coalitions for specific political objectives (Nelson 1979).[1]

---

[1]The solidarity of the Mathare Valley brewers, as Nelson has underlined, derives both from their common economic involvement and from the active hostility they face together from the outside society.

48

In some aspects of their self-reliance, the Mathare Valley beer-brewers are not unlike market women in many parts of the world. Market women frequently have well established networks, and their informal associations help them regulate the market. The extensive literature on market women points to many ways in which women's informal associations are important: in setting prices, planning market organization, patrolling market hygiene, punishing transgressors of market rules, establishing credit, and so forth.[2]

In general, it appears that women's esteem and influence in most communities are closely connected with the extent of their extra-domestic associational ties, many of which have clear economic roots and purposes. Both Lewis, in her discussion of Ivoirian market women (1976), and Sutton and Makiesky-Barrow in their study of a Barbados town (1977), have stressed this point. Abidjan market women go to great lengths to widen their outside associations, both by joining semi-formal voluntary groups and by reinforcing their kinship networks -- often with money contributions. This, they are well aware, enhances their autonomy, their status in the community, and hence their bargaining power vis-a-vis their husbands (Lewis 1976). In Barbados, too, the autonomy of women as well as men increases as their social involvements grow. While their extra-domestic associations can be with members of both sexes, women's single-sex networks in Caribbean cultures have been underrated (Sutton and Makiesky-Barrow 1977).

An awareness of the full impact of informal economic associations on women's management of their economic resources thus results in a richer and more accurate depiction of the division of power between men and women. Knowledge of these associations is important to analysts and planners seeking to allocate resources between women and men in ways that fit the social setting but neither tip the balance of power between the sexes nor contribute to the consolidation of any other unified single bloc within the community.

What, then, are the patterns of women's active economic informal associations? The outlines of an active women's political economy are traced by the design of women's informal associations, including the lines drawn by kinship and residence. But, the basic scaffolding that upholds women's economic strategies is built in turn upon their resources, such as the property women inherit, and constraints, such as those structured by sexual divisions of labor. These are the elements that shape the ways in which women organize themselves and their labor. This simple starting point for evaluating the bases of women's autonomous economic action unearths a wealth of information. Not only is there a voluminous literature on both the sexual division of labor and sex differentials in property rights, but, ultimately, property and labor rights constitute the basic limits on sex differences in economic opportunity.

---

[2]See especially Little 1973: 50-60, and also the following discussions on both rotating credit and ritual associations.

Property Rights

Property is a principal means to economic security and advancement. Even, or perhaps especially, when shares are small, variations in the size and nature of an endowment drastically alter abilities to save, invest, profit, and, above all, survive. As people endeavor to protect or improve their position, and finally to pass on a viable economic base to their children, they must constantly make decisions about the property they control. Depending upon the kind and extent of that property —land, pigs, or earrings, a lot or a little — they will face different economic opportunities and pitfalls as well as acquire varied skills.

Women and men typically inherit and control different economic resources. The kind of property that individuals control affects not only the economic resource base with which they must work but also patterns their economic associations with others. Friedl (1967) argues that women who receive land from their parents not only create a different productive base for themselves and their families, but also shape communities. Their continued involvement with land and with agricultural decisions in their natal communities necessitates strong intercommunity alliances for women. This gives women a great deal of political and economic leverage both where they were born and where they marry.

Generally, however, women in much of the third world do not receive endowments of real property; women more typically inherit movable property such as jewelry, produce, money, and other goods. In a provocative piece of research, Mintz argues that movable property displays an investment potential quite distinct from that of land and other real property. It is precisely because women's traditional property can be bought, sold, loaned, or invested more flexibly than land, Mintz (1971) suggests, that so many more women enter trade and subsequently establish market alliances with other similarly enterprising woman traders. Thus, when men and women inherit different types of property, they must capitalize upon the varying potentialities of those properties, acquire different skills, and enter different economic alliances.

Not only does the kind of property an individual receives have an important influence upon the character of economic associations, but the way in which it is obtained also affects the overall pattern of economic relationships in any given community. The channels through which property is transmitted shape culture-specific forms of economic solidarity by encouraging people to maintain some relationships and abandon others. For example, siblings of both sexes who share rights in the property of both parents, as is the case in much of Polynesia, must maintain cooperative and exchange relations with one another throughout their lives in order to retain their productive base. Similar patterns of cross-sex sibling alliance commonly recur when both inherit from a shared source. In indigenous Andean communities, on the other hand, where women inherit from their mothers and men from their fathers, a system of parallel but separate inheritance creates two sex-distinct paths of material obligation, and same-sex alliance is strong (Bolton and Mayer 1977).

Throughout the developing world, the major difference in the ways women and men inherit property is that men usually inherit at parental death or retirement while women tend to receive their entitlement at marriage. Confusions about the implications of this contrast abound, and cloud our understanding of the implications for women of the two predominant traditions for the transfer of property rights at marriage -- dowry and bridewealth.

Dowry is often taken as a sign that women are devalued, as a material bribe that fathers must pay to incite young men to accept otherwise worthless brides. A closer inspection of dowry practices, however, reveals a very different reality. Dowry does not reward men for supporting wives; it is, as Friedl (1967) shows, an endowment placed in trust for a couple's future progeny. Dowry, then, is a way of consolidating affluence across generations; it both stems from and supports class-based stratification (Goody and Tambiah 1973). Because strategies of upward class mobility often also force the privatization of women's place, demands for dowry may indirectly devalue women. The essential culprit, though, is not any underlying cultural stereotype for the worthlessness of women but an obsessive aspiration for class mobility and prestige forms of wealth.

An analogous argument can be framed for bridewealth (see again, Goody and Tambiah 1973). Rather than marking a greater worth of women, bridewealth (formerly called 'brideprice'), like dowry, enmeshes couples and their marriages in wider community economic relations that endure through subsequent generations. Instead of creating linear family trusts as does dowry, bridewealth circulates wealth laterally, through sibling sets and into an extended kin group (Krige and Krige 1943). Both bridewealth and dowry are systems of economic surety for new marriages: where class wealth is the presumed guarantor of dowried women's marriages, extended kin- and sibling-solidarity protect the marriages of women in bridewealth systems.

Class, family, or kin group stability, not women's economic security, are at issue in the contrast between dowry and bridewealth. The extent to which women's economic position and associations are materially affected by such practices hinges not only on the class and kin implications of dowry and bridewealth as systems for establishing economic solidarities. The effect on women depends ultimately on whether or not women themselves obtain control of any property, and if so, what kinds, and through what relations.

In some societies, whether through dowry, bridewealth, or direct inheritance, women may obtain and be responsible, for example, for domestic animals. In such cases, women must organize stud or fosterage exchanges. They may have to determine pasture or water rights and organize their labor to provide daily fodder and water. They may control sale of animals or their products and determine reinvestment plans. In other societies, women may inherit land, which is likely to involve them in agricultural decisions, or movable wealth, which might encourage them to enter trade. In each of these cases, constructive development planning would at first depend upon ascertaining what property belonged to whom before setting about to improve productivity, since sex differences can so easily be exacerbated by altering the value of the property of one sex but not the other. Yet many otherwise well-conceived development efforts founder, and ultimately have a negative impact upon women, for precisely this reason: the failure to consider sex-based differentials in property rights.

A pilot Food and Agriculture Organization (FAO) project for small farmers begun among the Tamang in Nepal in 1976-77, for example, was designed to supplement on-farm income for families with insufficient land for subsistence. The FAO hoped to help stem the flood of displaced rural migrants to the cities by making the minimal farm existence less marginal. Since land was limited, this FAO project turned to animal husbandry. It established cooperatives for the male heads of households and provided them with loans for the purchase of animals. Unfortunately, neither the FAO advisers (based in Thailand) nor their Nepalese intermediaries (who were from an ethnic, religious and linguistic group different from the Tamang) thought to inquire about the traditional sexual division of property according to which, among the Tamang, land is inherited by men and livestock primarily by women. The FAO loans of money, therefore, not only went into male hands that were less experienced in matters of animal husbandry, but also — had the intervention been successful — would eventually have undermined the very basis upon which Tamang women build their economic counterweight vis-a-vis men.

Establishing which sex controls what resources may not always be easy. In some ethnographic instances, for example, women may not have direct control of many or any significant resources. Inheritance rules may systematically pass over daughters in favor of sons, so that one must probe deeper to uncover women's residual economic resources. Systems of dowry and bridewealth vary dramatically in the extent to which they provide independent economic surety to women. Women may also receive 'gifts' as their economic entitlement over a longer period or at many various prescribed times in their lives. In such situations, although male inheritances may constitute the most obvious productive economic base, women's wealth, however it is obtained, should not be ignored. Sometimes, it may almost equal the male endowment in cash value. Thus, the composite value of a woman's jewelry, her household goods, domestic animals, and perhaps cash may be essentially equivalent to the value of her husband's house, land or herds. Her wealth may not routinely feed or house the family, but it often constitutes an important investment against age, inflation, illness, or family emergency.

In other instances, a woman may actively parlay her wealth into marked improvements in the family's basic living. A poor Tamang woman, for example, was given a small amount of money — one anna (a now defunct coin worth 1/16 of a rupee) — in the days (as she said) when "money wasn't cheap like it is today." She gradually transformed this minuscule endowment into enough money to buy the land on which one of her sons now lives with his wife and children. As she summarized it:

I bought thread for 1/16th of a rupee a skein and wove a man's turban. For that turban I got 2 1/2 rupees. I left 1/2 rupee with my mother, than I took the other 2 rupees to the Tibetan border (to trade for salt). On the way to the Tibetan border I found corn at 3 gallons for 1/2 rupee, so I bought 12 gallons and came back home within 9 days [i.e. quickly]. I loaned out the 9 gallons of corn [sic — or did they eat the rest?] in badiya [a common type of loan among women on which interest is paid in grain each year]. Then later I collected on those loans in full and took the grain to Kathmandu where I sold it for 20 rupees. Then with that money and a little more I had accumulated I bought the land that my middle son is now living on for 25 rupees (March: personal communication).

By 1977, when she told her story, the land she bought then was worth about 5000 rupees and so represents no small improvement over the original one anna she started with. Similar tales abound, not only among the Tamang, but in many parts of the world.

Sexual Divisions of Labor

Such examples not only demonstrate the importance of learning which sex controls what kinds of property, but also underscore the significance of traditional sexual divisions of labor. Often the main economic resource available to women is their own labor. The Tamang woman in the above example began her climb up the economic ladder by profiting from women's traditional labor, weaving.

Ironically, when the planners of the FAO Tamang small farmers project learned about the women's ownership of livestock and wanted to correct the possible sexual imbalance their project had introduced, they chose to lend money for the purchase of thread. They instituted an auxiliary program to make loans of up to 300 Nepalese rupees available to 'small farmer' households specifically for domestic weaving. Three hundred rupees was an amount approximating the total average annual cash income of these families at that time. The FAO planners neither determined whether there were markets for handwoven Tamang cloth, nor did they make any provisions for expanding that market. But, even more immediately critical, the planners did not learn that the profit margin on locally produced woven goods, even if a market were found, was not enough to meet the 12-13% annual interest charged by the FAO project, especially since an (illegal) 10% 'administrative tax' was typically raked from the top of development loans by local project intermediaries. Moreover, the FAO project administrators chose to make loans to the weavers' husbands, although the labor and marketing obligations for repayment fell upon the women weavers themselves. As March's field notes at the time indicated:

> ...there is no profit at all in this development weaving enterprise. More important, perhaps, are the potential effects of this ill-thought-out scheme on women and the women's world. At present, weaving is an exclusively women's domain. Weaving is undertaken on the woman's own initiative, with her own capital and for her own profit, and, most significant, perhaps, to reinforce the ties of her own social universe. In short, at present, women weave to satisfy their own needs. They weave for themselves, for their families and especially for their daughters, or as gifts for their own friends or special kin. When they weave for sale, it is generally to raise money for their own purposes, as in the case of (a particular mother and daughter) who were doing a great deal of weaving to pay for the daughter's divorce.

> This is not, of course, to say that the whole family of a weaver doesn't benefit or that women do not, at times, weave for the family's general welfare. (There) are obvious examples of almost landless families who manage to make ends meet primarily through the weaving efforts of the women. But in no case is the woman forced into the position of producer of petty cash for general familial needs so directly as she will be by the newly instituted "small farmer's" loans. In the first instance, the money is not ever

really hers: it is loaned to the male head of her household and will undoubtedly be (at least partially) used to meet the general cash needs — from bazaar-bought clothing to salt and cigarettes -- of the household. (Since the money comes into his hands first and even though Tamang husbands and wives are generally very cooperative, these expenditures will be made) at the man's more than the woman's discretion, while the obligation to repay the loan falls entirely on the woman.

Depending upon the extent to which the women retain control of the loaned money and its uses, the program may be more or less exploitative. At its worst, it could be the institutionalization of a husband's right to commandeer his wife's earnings for his own purposes and her obligation to provide him with a cash income from her own labors. At its best, because a woman's weaving time is limited, it nevertheless precludes women's maintenance of their own networks and simultaneously transfers the center of control away from them, while leaving them with the exclusive responsibility for providing the labor (March field notes, April 19, 1977).

The historical record is replete with examples where intervention shifted the sexual balance to disadvantage women in the division of labor (see especially Etienne and Leacock 1980; Hafkin and Bay 1976). The result has often been not only to undercut women's resources for economic parity with men, but even to increase the women's labor obligations.

Predominant among such disruptions were the cash crops introduced in many colonial countries. Beginning with Boserup's study (1970), many authors have reported the continuing erosion of women's economic security as the traditional division of labor for subsistence was transformed. Colonial policies which standardized private ownership titles to land, usually in the hands of men, destroyed women's rights to land under traditional communal or family ownership (Okeyo 1980; Romalis 1979). They established cash crops and cash income possibilities which were open only to men (Tinker 1976). Hays shows in well-documented detail how the combined policies of colonial states and missionary churches created a "nearly impossible situation," the real burden of which "in the rural areas of western Kenya fell on the women, who remained at home while their husbands and sons sought outside employment" (1976: 87). Such disregard for former sex differences in property rights and labor have made women's lives, as Huston's interviews describe quite poignantly, more difficult than before (1979).

Just as it is not always easy to get accurate information regarding the kinds of property men and women separately control or how each controls it, so, too, much of the information about the sexual division of labor is submerged. It is obscured, first of all, by a literature which has taken people's idealized statements about what each sex should do at face value, as true and objective statements about what the sexes actually do. Thus, that literature, as well as the many subsequent debates about the reasons or origins for universal patterns in the sexual division of labor, is only partially useful to the development planner. It represents idealized conceptions about the proper interdependence of the sexes and the place of gender in the moral world order; as such, its resemblance to economic reality varies greatly.

Some statements about what women and men should or should not do constitute real moral and economic imperatives that neither the individuals in that society nor those interested in development can lightly dismiss. Others are more flexible. Thus, the Tamang say both that men should not weave women's skirts and that it is women's work to haul water, but although men never weave, they frequently assist with water carrying. The femaleness of weaving is integral to the Tamang conception of the mythic origins of human society, but the hauling of water is more or less just another task. Obviously, simple lists of men's work and women's work would not suffice to differentiate between those tasks which are always and only the tasks of one sex, from those in which crossover is permissible under certain circumstances (Dyson-Hudson 1960) or again, from those in which typical behavior is not highly sex-specific at all, normative claims notwithstanding.

One of the most common constraints upon the sexual division of labor is childcare. Many of the studies on the impact of childcare obligations upon women's work opportunities suffer from the failing discussed above (Brown 1969; Nerlove 1974), but it remains undeniable that where children are women's work, shared childcare practices free women to engage in other activities. The very patterns of available childcare itself effectively constrain women's employment options (Stack 1974; Young and Willmott 1962). Petty employment, piecework, or other such limited forms of part-time employment may both be made possible by mutual childcare arrangements (Bujra 1979) and be limited to those forms if only sporadic and part-time childcare is available. Permanent migration, long distance marketing, or regular wage employment appear to be dependent upon equally long-term forms of childcare (Dubisch 1977).

In sum, what is needed, before the economic importance of the active strategies undertaken by women's informal associations can be well understood, is a detailed grasp of the kinds of economic resources women are likely to control and a precise sense of the obligations women are expected to meet with those resources. Stylized or stereotypic reports cannot provide this kind of information. Once the material baseline for women's economic action has been established through field observations and inquiries, it is possible to move on to questions regarding equity in women's informal associations themselves and their potential in planned change.

ROTATING ASSOCIATIONS

There are two major types of informal associations among economically active women that warrant discussion in some depth here: rotating work groups and rotating credit associations. We have chosen to consider these two for several reasons. Often, the ethnography of women's associations shows more diversity than similarity, but both rotating labor and credit associations can be found in many parts of the developing world. In addition, insofar as the concept of 'development' is taken to be nearly synonymous with 'economic development,' rotating credit and labor associations are among the most pointedly economic of informal associations. Moreover, among the many economically active informal associations found in the developing world, these rotating unions demonstrate the highest degree of equality and reciprocity in the ways in which they distribute resources, leadership, and decision making. There appears to be a 'bonus' advantage, as well, in considering rotating associations: in these associations, women commonly predominate, although men are rarely explicitly excluded. Among the many forms of female solidarity found around the world, rotating associations tread a delicate path, primarily serving women but without espousing sexual separatism.

Rotating Labor Associations

The most important principle underlying all examples of exchanged labor is the concept of reciprocal aid. At its most informal, mutual aid can be directly reciprocal — as, for example, between two women friends, co-residents, or neighbors, who pool their energies in daily labors such as husking, winnowing, or grinding grains. Around the world, the image of two or three women alternating pestle blows into a large mortar for pounding grains is commonplace, as is that of women winnowing or grinding together. Such exchanges operate on a largely uncalculated, but implicitly reciprocal basis: each woman helping others in exchange for help herself. The principle of mutual aid embodied in these exchanges can inform development planning, but these most minimal examples do not provide a widely replicable model. Better models can be derived from the more complex reciprocal labor forms we shall here call rotating labor associations.

Rotating labor is one of the most widespread forms of human cooperation. In almost all societies there are at least some tasks for which the labor of the domestic unit is insufficient. Except in highly monetized economies, where all labor outside of the family is paid, most cultures recognize some contexts in which people cooperate to exchange collective labor. They band together to work at the task needed by one of their party, all in the full expectation that their efforts will eventually be reciprocated as the group reassembles to perform work for each participant in turn.

Sometimes these tasks are relatively infrequent and the cycles of rotation slow. Udy suggests that we call this type of reciprocal labor palihog, after the Bisayan Filipino term, or gloss it in English 'discrete reciprocity' because it is usually called upon for discrete tasks, "the amount of work to be done is diffuse, and the time and occasion for reciprocation indefinite, although reciprocation is definitely expected" (1959: 78). We might also call this form of slow rotational labor 'the work party' because of the way in which it commonly operates.

In the work party, an individual or household in need of assistance calls in friends, neighbors, and relations for some particularly labor-intensive task, such as rice transplanting, clearing new fields, harvesting at peak seasons, or house building. Typically, the work party is feasted but not actually paid for their labors. The sponsor assumes that she or he will be asked to participate in a reciprocal work party at some time, but the exchange is casual and open-ended.

There are many reasons why cooperative labor might be relatively rare or the cycles of reciprocity long in any given society. The ecology of some people's livelihood requires dispersed residence, as among traditional camp-living Eskimos. Eskimo cooperation appears to be (or to have been) restricted largely to the nuclear household, the labors of wife, husband, and children sufficing the family without need for much routine assistance from kin and neighbors (Briggs 1974). Besides times of famine, when people band together to pool hunting skills and resources, according to Mirsky, "Eskimo cooperation is found principally in the whale hunts and shark roundups (formerly in reindeer and musk-ox drives), and to a lesser degree in the building and organizing of their winter houses. Yet within this cooperative framework an extraordinary amount of individualistic play is found" (1961: 56). Mirsky compares this cooperation to "a federation of sovereign states, composed of members who can join or not at will" (1961: 56).

An analogous emphasis on individual autonomy probably contributes to the relative infrequency of cooperative labor among other groups of people, such as the Sherpa of Nepal (March 1979) or the people of Mt. Hagen in New Guinea (M. Strathern, 1972). Even so, both among the Sherpa and Mt. Hageners, there remain some tasks, such as housebuilding and cooking for large communal feasts, which require more labor than a single person or household can provide. Among the Sherpa such occasions give rise to collective labor, called ngalok, which can be theoretically called together for any kind of work; in practice, however, communal labor generates sufficient tension that it is called upon only when the work load is unavoidably exceptional, as in house-raisings. Even then, an exact tally of labor contributed is kept, and people are careful to reciprocate precisely, although the time elapsed before repayment can be considerable (March 1979).

Even such sporadic cooperative labor has features which make it an interesting, if limited, model for planned social change: in the words of the Eskimo anthropologist, "all these are cooperative enterprises in which the work and the rewards are shared by the whole community" (Mirsky 1961: 56). These work parties should be interesting to planners since they are both informal and actively cooperative, involving, as Herskovits has indicated, "the voluntary association of a group of men or women whose objective is the completion of a specific, definitely limited task, with which they are simultaneously concerned" (1965: 100). As models for change, however, they lack the capacity for continuity. Although they could perhaps provide an adequate design for one-shot development efforts, such as the building of a local water supply system or road, they do not provide for sustained cooperative effort, such as is necessary for the maintenance of those systems or roads.

The kind of reciprocal aid which provides the greatest potential for more sustained development planning is found not in the work party so much as in the informal rotating labor association. A rotating labor association is one in which all the members converge to assist each of their number in rotation for specific tasks. Tasks performed by rotating labor associations may be large or small, predictable or unforeseen, agricultural or domestic — in short, they confound many of the same distinctions implicitly drawn in the common contrast between public and private. For these reasons, although most ethnographic accounts mention rotating labor exchanges, few have developed a good conceptual framework for understanding their unique strengths. They are able to combine the sociability of working in groups, the effectiveness of larger labor pools and the reliability and endurance of a prescribed rotational pattern, with the flexibility and mutuality of informal organizational structure. Some rotating labor associations consist of relatively bounded groups where the same people meet repeatedly to assist each member. Another common pattern is for each person to possess a series of dyadic, reciprocal labor obligations, so that no two labor associations are the same although their membership may overlap extensively.

Following Udy (and the Bisayan Filipino) once more, this type of ongoing work group might be called bolhon or 'rotational reciprocity:' "The distinguishing features of the bolhon are that reciprocity occurs in rotation among the participants, with each participant serving as manager/proprietor in turn and receiving the same amount of work as measured by some relatively explicit standard, usually time or spatial area. All reciprocal obligations are thus automatically discharged in the course of a single complete 'rotation'" (1959: 77). Reciprocity here is balanced within a clear time span rather than remaining diffuse and open-ended. Ethnographic accounts of such everyday rotational reciprocity are comon — so common, in fact, that it is impossible to survey their distribution throughout the world briefly. They can be found almost everywhere in the less mechanized and less monetized world.

In Africa, for example, Kaberry describes the Bamessi 'working-bee,' called tzo, saying it

> consists of women, who are of about the same age and who are kin or friendly neighbors. For the preparation of corn beds there may be ten or twelve individuals; for weeding only three or four. About a week's notice is given and, once a woman has received help on her own plot, she is under an obligation to fulfill a similar duty to others on pain of being reported to the Fon (chief). The women usually work in pairs, sing, chat, and urge each other on. Towards the end of the afternoon a small repast is provided, which includes a little fish contributed by the husband. In Ngie a team (mbu) ranges in size from three to eight for farms adjacent to the village, but is larger for those in the bush... The women hoe with zest, and often pointed out to me the saving in time and the pleasure of companionship. 'We have joined together to work because we are not strong. If we work together, we finish very quickly' (1952: 56).

Kaberry cites the presence of similar 'working-bees' among a number of other African groups: "The same word is used in Ngwo (mbo?); but in Beba the term is ifii; in Bentsan — ekwi'ake; in Koshin — tingala; in Fang — kengera; in Fungom village — andji'awo; in Zhoaw — tezam; in Aghem — zem; in Bali — nsu; in Mfumte — junkap; and in Mbem — bofak" (1952: 56 fn). Among the Bathonga of South Africa, too, Goldman describes the use of rotating mutual aid in preparing and planting the fields:

> The work must be done hastily to take advantage of the last rains. To facilitate matters, a woman whose fallow ground is beyond her own capacity to work will invite her neighbors to a djimo [working party]. Such invitations are willingly accepted, for not only has the woman prepared large jugs of beer, but her neighbors know that they can depend upon her assistance when they in turn need it (1961: 356).

In the Pacific, the most widely cited case involves women's cooperative production of tapa cloth (cf. esp. Herskovits 1952: 499), where groups of women each contribute sections of partially processed tapa to a collective finishing effort. Goldman also documents reciprocal agricultural labor among the Philippine Ifugao where "the arduous back-straining work in the hot tropical sun" of tending the rice fields between trans-planting and harvest is done as "groups of women cooperate to do the fields of one and then of another" (1961: 155).

In Asia, there are several detailed accounts of rotational mutual aid. In Nepal, for example, most reports at least mention parma (as it is called in Nepal) labor exchange, although it may be called by a variety of terms in the many languages of Nepal. Parma is a type of rotational labor exchange which is particularly well suited to the labor needs of marginal peasants in situations of the kind of climatic and ecological variability found in mountain Nepal.

It appears to be most widely practiced by households who have approximately enough land for their own subsistence needs; without any surplus production, these households neither have need for much supple-mentary labor, nor have the means to reimburse it. Yet there are variations, not only in the precise distribution of available labor among households, but also in their labor needs at any particular time. In any given household, a normally hearty worker may be temporarily ill, recently in childbirth, or otherwise absent from the household labor force. Since rotating labor exchanges can function well with each household contributing only one person's labor, even households with less than their full complement of workers can participate effectively; few houses are ever so decimated in personnel that there is no one able to work in the parma exchange. The net result, then, is that the parma exchange helps to iron out fluctuations in the availability of labor for its member households.

Rotational labor exchanges also help even out the peak labor demand times of the agricultural cycle. Intensive subsistence agriculture produces cyclic periods of peak labor demands, either in response to the agricultural work cycle itself or because of weather cycles affecting agriculture. At times, the labor requirements of transplanting, weeding, or harvesting exceed the abilities of the personnel in lone households to meet them. Rotational labor pooling makes it possible for people to expand the labor available to them during these peak periods. The mountain ecology of Nepal accentuates normal agricultural periodicity: in a single village, fields located on the upper or shady slopes can be 2-4 weeks behind the lower or sunnier fields. Thus, the rotational pattern established by parma exchange is able to mobilize a larger work force by shifting the location of their work around the community following the micropatterns of need.

Parma exchange group size appears to vary rather considerably. Among the Tamang, for example, such groups in Tamang called nang, range in size from less than 10 to over 30 workers representing between 6 and 17 households. Typically, some 10 households pooling about 20 workers make up a nang (or parma) exchange labor group (March 1979).[3] Membership is fluid from year to year, but remains very stable in any one year or agricultural seasonal cycle. Although group membership is recruited within kin and, particularly, neighborhood or hamlet, the actual size of the group reflects both the scale of the participants' landholdings and the kind of agriculture being practiced or crop in question. Rotating

---

[3]Rarely, however, do all of the 20 available workers work simultaneously, so that the participating force is commonly between 10-15.

labor exchange groups, such as those found among the Tamang, then, make the most productive use of minimal resources by taking advantage of agricultural periodicity. They capitalize upon that periodicity by matching its fluctuations with their own pooled and concentrated labors.

The various features of all of these forms of rotating labor, whether personal exchanges, work parties, or rotating labor associations, constitute a creative model for development planning. They are indigenous forms of organization which do not invoke powerful hierarchies of authority in order to accomplish their work. Local legitimacy of these associations derives from a structure which guarantees that each member profits more or less equally from their collective efforts. In addition, rotational labor patterns around the world are able to vary in response to shifting ecological or occupational needs.

In addition, women appear particularly active in rotating labor, yet the organizational form itself does not ideologically exclude men. Although the form tolerates considerable sexual segregation, in keeping with cultural expectations in many societies, it need not be organized expressly around that segregation. Even in the absence of specific ideological tenets regarding the segregation of women or female solidarity, rotating labor groups involve large numbers of women, help them utilize their labor and resources most effectively, and create the organizational base for further social and economic advancement.

In Nepal, for example, Pignede, speaking of the composition of nogar rotating labor exchange groups among the Gurung, discusses the system of exchange at some length in terms of both men and women before he indicates: "Between 15 and 19 years of age, young men are the majority in the nogar; then their numbers diminish abruptly...Women begin to work in the nogar when they are a little less than 17 years old. After 19, they are much more numerous than the men" (1966: 129 [March translation]).

While there are examples of all-male rotating labor associations in the world, many of the reported instances are described as being either mixed-sex cooperative groups (wherein the sex ratio, when specified, often favors women) or all-female. We might logically suspect labor pooling to be a more immediately essential adaptation for women. The kind and amount of property that women control often make women's economic security far more dependent upon labor-intensive efforts than men's. Moreover, rotational labor exchange appears ethnographically to be a strategy of the economically marginal, and more women than men fall into that category. Given the spotty nature of the cross-cultural evidence, however, it would be premature to insist at this time that women have more frequent recourse to rotating labor groups than men overall. In any case, it is clear from the evidence that millions of women in the world organize their work around informal rotating labor exchanges.

It is also worth noting that these rotating groups frequently provide an economic power base for women and foster female solidarity without necessarily conceptualizing either that base or its solidarity in opposition to men's. Rotating labor associations, even when they are activated in the course of women's active economic strategies, do not necessarily invoke an ideology of sexual segregation. Unlike the many "women's programs" which have emerged in recent years to assist women exclusively, intervention within the context of informal rotating labor associations could possibly target women without further marking or isolating them.[4]

Rotating Credit Associations

In many ways, rotating credit associations are very similar to rotating labor associations. They are widely distributed geographically. They involve large numbers of women. They help organize the resources of people's economic strategies especially where those resources are minimal. And they are structured to protect the interests of all participants more or less equally.

Because they have been the object of more focused academic research and, especially thanks to a few extensive comparative studies (see S. Ardener 1964 and Geertz 1962 and the case studies they cite), it is possible to summarize the geographic distribution of rotating credit associations at least roughly. Ardener, in particular, documents the presence of rotating credit associations on all the continents. In Asia and the Pacific, she describes associations found in pre-revolutionary China, among the Chinese in both Sarawak and Malaysia, among Indians in Malaysia, among the Malays themselves, in Java, Timor, the Philippines, and in Hong Kong, India, and Vietnam. To those sources cited by Ardener from Asia and the Pacific, we might add: China (Gamble 1944), Japan (Embree 1946), the Eastern Highlands (Sexton 1980 a & b) and, if we extend the definition somewhat, the Western Highlands (Feil 1978) of New Guinea, as well as South Korea (Campbell and Chang Shick Ahn 1962). In the Americas, Ardener reviews reports of rotating credit associations in Barbados, Guyana, Jamaica, among Peruvian Indians, and among the descendants of Yoruba slaves in Trinidad. There is additional research indicating their presence among Mexican Americans in California (Kurtz 1973), as well as in Mexico (Kurtz 1973; Kurtz and Showman 1978). Ardener's review of the literature also finds some reports of rotating credit groups in England and Scotland.

Her evidence, however, is most extensive with regard to Africa, Ardener's own area of particular anthropological expertise. In West Africa, she documents associations in Nigeria, the Cameroons, Ghana, Sierra Leone, Dahomey, and the Republic of Congo; in Central and East Africa, she found rotating credit associations in both Zambia and Zimbabwe. She also reports their presence in the Sudan, Egypt (see also Nadim 1977), and South Africa. To Ardener's well-researched summation of African associations we can add Lewis' report of rotating credit in Abidjan, Ivory Coast (1976). There are undoubtedly many more examples; research on women's economic activities continues to reveal them everywhere (Hamalian 1974; Lee 1976).

With such detailed descriptions available in the literature, it is possible to abstract some general principles concerning rotating credit associations. Like rotating labor, the concept of rotating credit is based

---

[4]Such efforts would, of course, have to be monitored very closely to make sure that women continued to be reached; one can easily envision a scenario in which the sex ratio of informal rotating labor could shift away from women as men moved in to coopt the increasing endowments of the associations.

upon a collective effort in which all the members participate and from which each profits in turn. The number of participants varies, as does the time span of the rotational cycle, and the amount of money circulated. Although many more precise definitions have been generated to describe particular cases, Ardener provides a concise and adequate working definition: A rotating credit association is

> ...an association formed upon a core of participants who agree to make regular contributions to a fund which is given, in whole or in part, to each contributor in rotation (1964: 201).

The two aspects of rotating credit associations which Ardener calls "essential criteria" (1964: 201) -- rotation and regularity -- are precisely the two features which make them interesting to us here. 'Regularity' is a relatively simple notion. It refers to the ways in which any given association perpetuates itself. That is, the association agrees in advance upon the amounts of the contributions (and hence, the resultant fund), on the time intervals between levies, and on whether or not the association will endure for only one cycle or for several. For example, 10 hypothetical members might agree to contribute $10 every week, making a regular 10-week (or 10-member-contribution) cycle; in any given week's cycle, then, one member would collect the pooled fund of, in this example, $100. Members may decide to go through only one cycle, or they can choose to establish a more permanent association, cycling and recycling. In fact, rotating credit associations have been structured over a whole range of regular patterns, ranging from the] to 1-penny daily funds established among the market women of Ife (Bascom 1952: 64) to much more substantial amounts of money levied and circulated at far greater intervals. Size of fund and length of interval can be increased dramatically by sharply increasing the number of participants, as in the case of the rotating credit associations reported to Bascom which lasted 5-8 years even though contributions were made weekly — which would mean that some 200 members must have been involved (1952: 64).[5]

'Rotation' is a more complex issue but basically refers to the fact that each member contributes to a fund which each person receives in turn. In the case of the hypothetical $100 fund above, one member was selected at random to receive the whole pot each time it was levied. There are, however, a variety of more complex ways in which either the order of rotation or the rotation cycles themselves have been calculated: by lot, by traditional seniority rights, by members' needs, by divination, or by auction (see Ardener 1964: 211-213). But the basic principle dictates that each member must have received the collective fund once before anyone can receive it a second time.

'Rotation' is not without its problems, however. Compared to many types of informal economic associations that work openly to the greater advantage of some participants (patrons and mistresses, for example) at the expense of others (their clients and servants), the inequities found in rotating credit associations are minor. Nevertheless, these inequities should be looked at, not only because they could detract from the desirability of development intervention in any particular case, but since

---

[5]Another example is the 200-member daily 1-rupiah funds assembled in markets in Java (Geertz 1962: 428).

they may help us understand the reasons that one form of rotating credit association may be more successful than another.

There are two positions in the rotating credit association which involve an element of potential privilege: those members who receive the fund early in the rotational cycle, and the organizers. Organizers, in some associations, receive extra consideration. They may, for example, be entitled to claim the communal fund, not once per cycle, but twice (Kurtz 1973: 51; Bascom 1952: 68). Or, the organizer "may be required to make his contributions only in the form of feasts, while other members pay only in cash" (Smith 1899 cited in Ardener 1964: 211). In some instances, the organizers are not regular contributing members to the fund, nor are they entitled to draw from it in the rotational cycle, but they may borrow from the fund without interest at any time for their own personal business ventures, as long as they do not disrupt the smooth functioning of the association's rotation (Nadel 1942: 371-373). Or again, an organizer may receive a percentage of each fund levied (Anderson 1966: 335-336; Nguyen van Vinh, cited in Geertz 1962: 253).

In all of these cases, however, we should not overlook the responsibilities of the organizer(s) to protect the association's resources from defaulters. In the cundina reported by Kurtz, for example, the organizer claims the first fund before the rotation officially begins, but must keep it as surety against a defaulter. If there is a default, the organizer must make up the fund to the rest of the association (1973: 52). In other instances, organizer(s) are expected to advance fund contributions to members temporarily short of cash so that the regularity of the cycle will not be interrupted (Anderson 1966: 337), or to pressure contributors into keeping up with their payments perhaps by going around to all members to collect personally (Bascom 1952: 66). On balance, then, it seems reasonable to construe the slight advantage granted to organizer(s) as compensation for their role in protecting the rotational cycle from delay or default. Even in the most highly professionalized forms, such as those found in Vietnam where organizers undertake to start and sponsor rotating credit associations as a personal business proposition, Geertz points out that "genuine bondage to the association manager of the sort all to (sic) common to the private Indian or Chinese moneylender evidently does not occur" (1962: 254).

Another source of some inequity derives from the rotational cycle itself. In effect, those who receive the fund early in the cycle get an interest-free loan. Imagine, again, a 10-week cycle among 10 members contributing $10 each, with no special consideration given the organizer. Each week, one among their number will collect a fund of $100. The person who collects the first fund will have paid in only $10, but will be able to pay back the $100 'loan' in simple interest-free installments over the next 10 weeks. The person who does not collect until the end of the cycle will simply reclaim the $100 already put out, without profit of interest. Later recipients in effect finance the interest on funds that were withdrawn earlier; economically speaking, they might as well have secreted their money under a mattress.

Different associations around the world have adopted various methods for reducing this inequity. Sometimes the different needs of participants are taken into account so that those with the greatest need are allowed to draw on the fund first (Ardener 1964: 211-212). Sometimes new members or those of uncertain reliability are placed last in the rotation to protect against their absconding with the fund (Kurtz and

Showman 1978: 76). The most common simple method, however, is to determine rotational order by lot, creating a gamble against the interest, which may be perceived, depending upon the culture, as either exciting or disreputable (Ardener 1964: 212). Of course, the original inequity of the rotational orders eventually gets ironed out, if the rotating credit association endures through several cycles.[6] It is important to ascertain the ways in which any particular rotating credit association solves the problems of organizer privilege and rotational interest inequity. Rotating credit associations provide a clear model for a structure that attempts to protect the separate interests of its participants equally.

A third major feature of rotating credit associations, not explicitly highlighted by Ardener (1964) but which can be inferred from the literature, is the high proportion of women active in them. At first glance, the literature gives only sporadic and rather anecdotal consideration to the sex ratios. Geertz, for example, talking of the urban rotating credit associations in Vietnam observes, literally parenthetically: "The urban ho (rotating credit associations) are run by professional managers (who, it happens, are all women)..." (1962: 253). Some authors provide a little more information, like Kurtz and Showman, who say "most commonly, the persons who consistently organize regular tandas (rotating credit associations in Mexico) are housewives" (1978: 67). Of the 19 instances of rotating credit associations reviewed by Ardener specifying the sex of participants,[7] 16 occur exclusively or primarily among women (1964). Thus, for example, among the rural Nupe of Nigeria "although wives of (male) farmers used the system, farmers themselves did not, 'nor have they apparently ever done so'" (Nadel 1942: 271-273 In Ardener 1964: 205). In Malaya, "rotating credit associations are said to be found among women, but not among men, in Indian communities" (Sharma 1962: personal communication cited in Ardener 1964: 203), while, in the Sudan, rotating credit associations "appear to have started among members of the middle age-group of women in the central townships who wanted to collect sums to buy gold ornaments for their daughters' weddings" (Ardener 1964: 207-208). In short, although the information is far from complete at this time, rotating credit associations, even where they are not explicitly organized along sex lines, involve fairly significant numbers of women.

Based on the studies where available information is more complete, it is possible to suggest some reasons for women's participation in these credit associations. Disproportionate female representation may hinge on the ways members are recruited and their investments protected. Few rotating credit associations have the legal sanction of the societies in which they are found; formal jural-political authority is vested more exclusively in more formal banking systems and, as we have seen, is

---

[6]Some rotating credit associations have devised extremely complex means for balancing interest inequity. See, for example, the summaries of methods described by Ardener (1964: 213-215) and Geertz (1962: 250-252) including bidding for different places in the order and calculation of interest into the contributions in sequence.

[7]Unfortunately, Ardener does not comment on the sex composition of another 16 cases, so the statistical significance, strictly speaking, of our observation needs further verification.

primarily the domain of men. The greatest surety provided for investors in rotating credit associations derives from preexisting personal bonds of mutual obligation. Most rotating credit associations are organized along lines of either kinship or residence, except in the most modern (and generally urban) situations where occupation and workplace become important. Correspondingly, as we have seen, women are not only pivotal in the kin and residential organization of most communities, but interpersonally binding mutual obligations link women into their informal associations.

Bascom's observations on the Yoruba esusu rotating credit associations cast an intriguing light on the question of the predominance of women:

> Two types of esusu groups were differentiated by informants: those whose membership is open to anyone, although it may be drawn largely from the group of relatives inhabiting the compound of the founder; and those whose membership is restricted to the inhabitants of one compound. The restricted esusu groups are associated with the meeting of the wives of the compound, ipade obinrin ile, and the meetings of the daughters of the compound, ipade omo-(o) binrin ile, with the contributions and disbursement of the fund occuring at their regular meetings...Although the men of the compound hold similar meetings, ipade omo-(o) kunrin ile, they prohibit the formation of esusu within their groups because it is felt that the harmony of the compound, which is considered far more important than an esusu, might be disturbed if the esusu were to be 'scattered' (i.e. dissolved by default or fraud) (1952: 66-67).

The need for strong personal ties to keep a rotating credit association going favors groups defined by the traditional rights or obligations of kinship and residence. Moreover, conceptions of same-sex harmony in contrast to commonly perceived differences in men's and women's relative positions within compounds further favors female participation.

Another reason why women frequently turn to rotating credit associations may stem from the relatively greater marginality of women compared to men in many societies. Nearly twenty years ago, Geertz spoke strongly in favor of rotating credit associations as a 'middle rung' in development, or as an indigenous means for capital formation and the formalization of economic activities in the pursuit of modernization (1962). With the passage of time, however, he has been criticized on many fronts. Kurtz in particular has argued that rotating credit associations are not universally part of modernization or economic development. In fact, Kurtz points out that their presence among the ethnic poor in the U.S. and among the urban poor in developing nations suggests that "such associations provide little if any training for any category of the population for participation in the nation's economic institutions. Nor in the complex economic situations provided by the United States does the existence of the rotating credit association seem terribly important in economic development. Rather, the rotating credit association serves in this context, and perhaps in urban contexts generally, as an adaptive mechanism which provides an alternative to participation in the mainstream of such a society" (1973: 50-51).

The evidence on rotating credit associations shows that they occur with far greater frequency among poorer segments of the population, excluded from, ineligible for, or wary of, more formal financial institutions. The sense of personal and socially sanctioned obligation created by the association appears able to override many other everyday claims on a poor person's money and permits at least some accumulation. It seems to be, as Katzin has observed of Jamaican rotating credit, "a precarious", but, we might add, no less effective, "way to save money in a community where almost everybody is badly in need of cash" (1958: 438). Amidst the many pressures on the meager resources of the very poor, only the collective interpersonal sanctions of a rotating credit association may be able to assure even the most modest personal savings. To individuals with powerful competing sanctions on limited funds, "the concept of putting money away for a rainy day is incompatible with an economic climate that begins each day with the raising of gale warnings" (Kurtz 1973: 56).

Moreover, according to Ardener, the rotating credit associations are unlike other means of obtaining loans, since their social respectability protects the dignity of borrowers: "In a rotating credit association, the recipient of a fund, far from suffering loss of dignity, is often the member of honour at a feast or some other form of entertainment" (Ardener 1964: 221). Because, then, of their appeal in a subsociety, removed from the formal structures of society but not without a sense of dignity, it is perhaps not surprising that large numbers of women organize themselves into rotating credit associations.

A Model for Change?

To plan economic changes which will reach women, and help redistribute wealth equitably among poor women, then, those women's informal associations which actively promote the economic interests of all members should prove a good model to follow. Although the great worldwide diversity in women's informal associations makes it difficult to identify such model associations without specific regional ethnographic and historical knowledge, two types of active associations -- rotating labor associations and rotating credit associations -- appear not only to exhibit the desirable characteristics, but also are found worldwide.

Rotating associations such as those we have reviewed here are generally based upon interpersonal ties of mutual obligation. Accumulation of labor or capital is difficult for people with marginal economic resources and many responsibilities; too many demands already compete for the time and money of the poor. Many women survive in their juggling of these demands by depending upon informal mutual aid networks. The interpersonal bonds underlying those informal associations are so crucial to the survival of marginal women that the claims they make on those women's resources can be effective at creating pools of capital or labor where any other more formal claim would fail.

Moreover, rotating associations simultaneously reach the economically marginal and affect them equally. As a form of economic organization, rotating associations do not allow any one participant to profit disproportionately. They rarely appeal to the wealthier strata, but instead serve middle and marginal people as indigenous forms of mutual self-help.

Finally, both types of rotating associations serve women in great numbers without stigmatizing either participants or associations as markedly female-segregated. Development efforts have largely failed women by ignoring their particular vulnerability and the unique organizational strengths that their position has generated, but development has also failed to reach many other classes of disenfranchised people as well. Rotating associations are promising especially because they reach women primarily without excluding others who are themselves equally excluded from formal opportunity — even though they happen to be men.

Because of all of these characteristics, rotating associations continue to be of great interest for the planning of locally responsive and sexually egalitarian development. Programs designed to reach women and others in the informal sectors of society and to help them improve their economic viability equitably, if they are to be successful, will undoubtedly share many structural and functional patterns with these rotating associations. But no association exists in a vacuum: it can be tied to the existing formal structures of society in many different ways, each of which will have distinct implications for outside intervention and the accessibility of informal associations to outsiders.

Moreover, although rotating associations are particularly intriguing because they are almost exclusively organized for the redistribution of economic resources, they also embody some important assumptions about collective action and the responsibility of leaders to the general membership. Effective economic development depends upon the simultaneous emergence of effective political organization. Yet, just as caution and careful observation are needed to create or reinforce active economic associations which are equitable sexually and otherwise, so it is essential to recognize differences in forms of political authority which may or may not be accesible to all women. The potential for rotating associations to serve as a model for intervention depends upon these wider constraints. It is to these that we must now turn to complete the picture of women's informal associations and their role in social change.

5

Women's Ritual and Religious Associations: Patterns of Authority and Power

Women's informal associations are not purely functional instruments for influence or change. Although they provide a collective basis for action — much of which has tangible economic, political, or social consequences -- they also express and consolidate women's cultural identities. The communal sanction of their constituencies, moreover, is not their only basis for legitimacy; religious and ritual associations, in particular, also draw upon a higher authority. They cast women's actions within a culturally meaningful frame, cloaking women's associations with an aura of spiritually inspired authority and orienting the place of gender in the wider world order. In ritual associations women actively exercise their authority as women within a divinely sanctioned interpretation of their gender rights.

Although women's ritual associations are improbable vehicles for direct economic development, these associations and the vision of authority they invoke are critical to thinking about change, since change both depends on and affects shifts in the traditional distribution of societal authority. Within the development fraternity, 'women's religiosity' has usually been conceived as an entirely conservative mechanism, a major force behind the perceived resistance of women to change. We will argue that a more subtle understanding of women's participation in religious and ritual associations, together with a recognition of the overall autonomous integrity of religious systems, show a more complex dynamic.

This interpretation of women's ritual solidarity highlights the political vitality of religious associations. In keeping with the more concrete purposes of this study, we may, for example, ask whether the authority vested in women's ritual associations primarily rationalizes their place in a wider conception of a sex-stratified world, or whether women's religious authority endows their sodalities with a legitimate basis for autonomous action. In this regard, our questions highlight distinctions like those drawn between active and defensive economic associations. The many examples we shall discuss (and the many more we do not) demonstrate the importance of such groups and associations as domains in which women legitimately acquire organizational and political skills.

We will ask a variety of questions about the structure of religious authority, about the nature of leadership in women's religious and ritual associations, and about the nature of member participation. The focus is on the distribution of political skills and resources within religious associations. These questions are analogous to the questions we have already asked about the distribution of material resources in economic associations. We can learn, for example, whether the rights of all members are equally protected, whether all members have equal access to the skills and places of decision making, or whether the privileges of authority become disproportionately vested in the hands of a few.

There are many perspectives from which women's solidarity in ritual associations might be approached. Ours is conceived in direct relation to its applications for economic planning. Speaking of religious associations in this way not only challenges the usual perception of the role of ritual and religion in society, but also forces refinement of the categories established by our analysis thus far. The conceptual contrasts that we have outlined — the distinctions between defensive and active strategies or between equity and privilege — are not immediately suited to the study of religious phenomena. Religious authority is not a political resource in the same way that labor or capital are economic resources. Nor are the distribution patterns of the two analogous. Although the authority of religious associations can give rise to activities that are undeniably political, religious associations are not themselves political institutions: their authority derives not from the polity but from a religious world view which may bear very little resemblance to our own more secular conception of authority. Furthermore, women's religious vision of authority may be simultaneously revolutionary and conservative, since many contradictory threads run through any religious system.

It is because of these very anomalies that we have included women's ritual associations in this study. There are two important points here: women's ritual associations not only shed light on women's political base, informing our understanding of the distribution of societal authority, but they also introduce important nuances into our categorization of informal associations as defensive or active, expressive or instrumental. In religious associations, more than most others, women's authority can emerge from the supposedly 'affective' basis of their shared cultural perceptions. On the other hand, women's religious associations can simultaneously protect and challenge traditional authority. Like the cultural and religious belief systems about gender to which they are tied, the social impact of women's ritual alliances is everywhere ironic and complex.

RESISTANCE AND CHANGE

Religion is often seen as an exclusively conservative force in women's lives. Religious dicta place limits on acceptable behavior and the religious idiom imputes to those dicta an immutability derived from the permanence of the sacred world order itself. Seen in this light, women's religious associations are primarily defensive: women turn to them in reaction to other limits placed on their activities. Accounts from around the world have portrayed women's religious involvement as compensation for their exclusion from other domains of activity. For example, after a lengthy discussion of Hindu women's religious activities in North India, where she describes a rich array of life-cycle rites, calendrical rites, shamanic consultations, and pilgrimages, Luschinsky concludes:

Religious activities appear to satisfy many needs of women, the need for emotional catharsis through spirit possession, the need for sociability, and the need for a sense of importance. Men have other ways of satisfying these needs. They can travel more freely than women when they want a change from the daily routine. Village politics and factionalism serve as outlets for their socializing in their evening hukka [smoking pipe] groups, which are spontaneous gatherings of men who enjoy each other's company after the sun has set. And men are well aware of their importance in this androcentric culture. Women must reassure themselves of their importance. Men make many decisions which affect women, and women sometimes have very little, if any, voice in the decisions. Aside from household work, religious activities provide the only opportunity for women to take initiative in major endeavors (1962: 718).

Luschinsky's report upholds the commonly held notion that women turn to religion because of all the other things they cannot do: if politics is for men, religion is for women.

An analogous argument is made about men's and women's differential participation in formal or public religion as opposed to informal or domestic religion. The formal religious institutions of priesthood, church, temple, or mosque, are typically in male hands. Women's greater activity in private, household, small-scale, or local religious events is often construed as a result of their exclusion from the more prestigious events.

Such a perspective on women's religiosity fails for reasons that are very like the failure to understand informal domains in general. First, contemporary western experience leads us to draw an overly sharp line between religion and politics. In most traditional communities, religion and politics are complexly interdependent; authority deriving from one sphere often brings authority in the other. Similarly, as shown in our discussion of the distinction between public and private domains (Chapter 2), the line between public and private ritual, or between formal and informal religion, cannot be sharply drawn in much of the world.

Finally, we cannot assume that there is a causal or logically precedent relation obtaining in the relations between formal and informal (or public and private) religion any more than we could assume that informal economic associations were a secondary or residual phenomenon relative to formal economic relations. Women's religious participation is not adequately described as behavior that is 'left over,' pushed out of the formal or political sphere by temporal processes, cultural notions of priority, or psychological fulfillment. Herein lies one of the most basic sources of confusion regarding women, religion, and change: either (1) that women's options are more conservative because their main avenues are religious (and religion is conservative), or (2) that religion is conservative because its most stalwart defenders are women (and women are conservative). We need not become engaged in the debate over causality here; the circularity of both of these presumptions derives from a similar perspective emphasizing the relative defensiveness of both religion and women — it interprets the workings of both negatively, with primary reference to what each is not or cannot do. Such a perspective suggests that religious pronouncements are primarily statements about what women should not do and that the main referent points in women's lives otherwise also hinge upon what they cannot do.

Women's lives are, of course, often seriously limited by religious ideologies that help rationalize those constraints. Yet, within whatever framework they are given, women lead complex and interesting lives, replete with undertakings far more assertive than we might initially assume. In this monograph our effort to understand the instrumental potential of women's informal associations has, perhaps, created an overly sharp dichotomy between active and reactive associations. The distinction remains important conceptually, especially when evaluating the implications for intervention in various circumstances. But a careful look at the bases for legitimacy and the active purposes of women's ritual associations forces us to recognize both the mutual permeability of our categories and the shifting dynamics of the tension between them. It requires us to question the basic relation between self-assertiveness and self-protection within women's informal strategies.

In order to do this, we must first recognize the independent structure and strengths of women's religious associations. In the words of Betteridge, an anthropologist who has worked with Muslim women, "women's religious activities are not a pale imitation of those engaged in by men" (1980: 142). Instead, she indicates, Muslim women's religious associations are varied and active, but structured differently from the formal religious events mainly sponsored by men. In particular, she discussed the rowzeh, or ritual meals offered in fulfillment of a religious vow. Although they are sometimes derided as "silly ladies' parties" even by Iranians (1980: 152), Betteridge shows that such evenings provide women with the opportunity to gather and discuss important events in their lives. As she points out, organization is informally structured around communication networks among women.

> Women, often lacking the extradomestic existence of men, are less likely to belong to organized groups that meet outside the home on a regular basis. This is not to suggest that women's activities are unstructured. Rather, women tend to use informal means in organizing and communicating with others about any ritual event. Women's ritual events are usually held in the home; news of them is spread through informal networks of family and friends. Women regard word of mouth as an effective means of publicizing a gathering. It is thought that news about gatherings for women should not be placed in public view. The large numbers of women attending the gatherings, and the still larger numbers aware of them, attest to the correctness of the women's assumption; formal publicity is unnecessary (1980: 142).

Leadership at these ritual meals is also not formally ranked or announced, but based on women's informal knowledge of each other's qualifications. The women who lead the prayers, recite religious stories, and direct sermons must know the scriptures, but they must also be women who can use their knowledge of religious accounts to comment on women's conception of their world. Thus, women use religious knowledge and the forum of ritual gatherings both to expound and to evaluate the constraints imposed on them by religion. One woman, who had been recommended highly to lead a ritual meal the year before, according to

Betteridge, had been very entertaining. She had told all those present that any women who did not make love with her husband when he wanted to would be hung by her breasts in hell. [One woman]'s apt comment to the women seated around her had been, 'If a man doesn't make love with his wife when she wants to, what do they hang him by?' [She] said that last year's rowzeh leader had been invited by mistake...A woman across the way laughed when she heard the story and told that she had come this year in hopes of hearing the same woman speak. An older woman next to me...told me not to believe what the woman had said about wives being punished in hell, because it probably wasn't true (1980: 149).

At these ritual meals, as in a host of other religious events organized and attended by women, the place of women in the orthodox religious world order is not simply enacted without criticism or comment, to become a template for women's opportunity. Women typically use such occasions to come to terms with that template: it is expounded, then exaggerated, then again contradicted, experimented with, sampled, savored, supported, and denied — all at the same time. Women's participation in informal ritual associations simultaneously works with, within, upon, and against the prevailing religious world view, including their own place in that view.

One case that makes this point and has risen to the forefront of much debate recently is ritual female circumcision.[1] In practices of female genital mutilation, as Rapp indicates, "We are confronted dramatically with the politics of tradition. Traditions may simultaneously give strength and provide insulation against radical revisions in women's often-contradictory position" (1979: 512). To the extent that we focus on the constrained and defensive nature of women's traditions, the extreme brutality of these operations confronts us. To the extent that we emphasize women's autonomy, it is also plain that the ritual associations which perpetuate such practices provide latitude for women's own political efforts. The contradiction between these two positions cannot be resolved by insisting upon the exclusive correctness of either. Ironic contradictions inhere in religion, ritual, and their place in women's lives.

The prevailing western perception of ritual female genital mutilation acknowledges no vision of political authority but a secular one, and therefore focuses on the pain and suffering of the initiates. From this perspective, women, deprived of personal control over their own sexuality, are forced by an apparently overwhelming consolidation of misogynist male power to participate in the rituals of their own oppression. Clitoridectomy and infibulation are thus seen as powerful instruments of social control, which ensure that women will be chaste, subordinate, and even unable to experience autonomous pleasure. The rituals initiate women, according to this view, to the uncompromising reality of their subordinate femaleness. While even this perspective must recognize that women themselves insist on the continued performance of these ritual operations, it sees the power and authority acquired by the female sponsors of ritual mutilation as reactionary and ultimately perpetuating the overall subjugation of women.

---

[1]For a view of the distribution and variation in practices of female circumcision and clitoridectomy, see WIN News, especially, Hosken 1978.

Such a perspective admits only one interpretation of both pain and authority; this is its weakness and its appeal. No analysis of these ritual initiation practices should erase or belittle the suffering involved (see especially Daly 1978: 154). At the same time, while all human neurosensory mechanisms for experiencing pain are universal, all pain is not perceived uniformly: cultural and religious systems can transmute the interpretation of pain extensively. To see firewalking, fasting, celibacy, vision quests -- or the countless other trials through which people pursue metaphysical goals -- as merely 'painful' is to miss their point.

Rituals of female genital mutilation are undeniably part of an overall belief system in which women's perceived hypersexuality necessitates drastic controlling measures. Nevertheless, it is not helpful to impose a purely secular notion of authority on circumstances wherein the religious and the political are inextricably intertwined; the conundrums of women's 'traditional religious conservatism' are more convoluted. Religious authority, reflected and reinforced by women's ritual associations, also legitimates considerable political action by women even though the limits to that authority are tied to the place of both gender and power in the overall religious world view.

RITUAL LEADERSHIP AND SECULAR POWER

At one level, informal religious and ritual associations can be seen as important opportunities for women to acquire political skills. The many positions of authority and responsibility for women within their religious and ritual associations give considerable experience in decision-making, administration, dispute-settlement, management of collective resources, staging of public events -- all activities requiring leadership and political skill. The authority women gain through their ritual associations extends their legitimacy into the formal secular politics of their society.

Some women's religious or ritual associations are closely linked to the formal spheres of political and economic authority in their society. Such associations are often among the most formalized of women's voluntary religious associations. In a study of Protestant women's associations in Freetown, Sierra Leone, Steady (1976) underscores the ways in which such associations directly support a tripartite status quo of the church, the male clergy, and the double standard of morality for men and women. The associations indirectly feed into the wider Freetown political and economic ethic of individual private enterprise by simultaneously promoting both self-improvement and benevolence. These Freetown associations resemble women's voluntary religious associations in many parts of the world; they serve prevailing social, political, and economic interests by relegating the impetus for change to individual initiative and charity.

Such associations represent the most formalized of religious groups and tend to be closely embedded within wider structures of formal relations — of class interest, political authority, or ethnic majority. Many religious and ritual associations are far more autonomous. Prayer groups, girls' initiation societies, spiritualist gatherings, religious reading and study groups, ritual feasting societies, spirit possession meetings, and religious curing sessions are but a few examples of arenas that do not directly depend on formal social structures of society. They can cross-cut family, class, ethnic, and local ties to create a partially independent basis for women's ritual -- or religious -- based solidarity.

Whether they legitimate a place for women's action within or alongside the status quo, however, all women's ritual and religious associations are alike in providing opportunities for female leadership. Channels of women's religious leadership that run parallel to male leadership are perhaps most explicit under Islam. There men and women are sharply segregated, and "the likelihood is greater that women will develop separate religious ceremonies and leaders" (Fernea and Fernea 1972: 391). Women do hold important religious offices that provide opportunities for religious leadership and display a wide array of Muslim activities. Women's popular gatherings for readings of the Koran appear to have the widest geographical spread, occuring in every community of Muslim women for which we have evidence.

The most prominent women's leaders at these gatherings are the mullah-s. Mullah-s are trained religious specialists who read from the Koran, preach, and guide the prayers of the women who attend. They are evaluated by and respected for both their expertise in written and oral tradition as well as their personal magnetism and inspiration in leading women's gatherings. Theirs "is a highly esteemed profession, and profitable as well — a gifted woman can support an entire family" (Fernea and Fernea 1972: 399). The lay women who organize, finance, and host these religious gatherings are also highly respected. Along with the mullah-s, they are focal personages in the women's community. They bring together informal and shifting associations of women not only to share news and gossip, but also to speculate upon the Koranic implications of their lives. Thus, the women who take part in these feasts, gatherings, and readings -- and especially their leaders -- sample not only the power of their sex-segregated communication networks, but may also invoke the authority of the Koran to support their positions.

Saints, shrines, and pilgrimage constitute another important domain fostering Muslim women's leadership. Women obtain considerable organizational and political experience by their various roles associated with the shrines. Dwyer indicates that "while mwasim, the major festivities in honor of saints, are generally organized by men, most ma'arif, the one-day local saintly festivities which far outnumber mwasim, are generally organized by women. The women of a neighborhood collect the money, prepare the food, invite the guests, and ultimately distribute the baraka or supernatural power" (1978: 587). The management of shrines engenders what Dwyer calls "a host of female functionaries, primary among them curers and muqaddamat (leaders and caretakers)" (1978: 587). Fernea and Fernea underscore the special importance of the nakiba, the female staff of shrines in Egyptian Nubia, both to the general shrine maintenance and to women on pilgrimage (1972: 396).

Religious leadership not only gives women experience directing the internal affairs of women's religious activities, but also "tends to command a large measure of automatic respect even outside the church hierarchy" (Steady 1976: 396). Among the Shahsevan nomads, who were described earlier, a woman who was a returned pilgrim was not only respected for her religious authority, but wielded considerable secular authority as well. Such a woman joined with the senior men to constitute the opinion leaders and judiciary of the community. "The opinions of such a woman in matters of family law and custom are sought by both men and women, and her advice is given equal weight with that of men" (Tapper 1978: 382). Tapper recounts one case in particular where "a betrothed girl was said to have been suckled by her fiance's mother, but no one could remember or would admit the extent to which this took place. It was therefore uncertain whether the engaged couple were foster siblings according to Islamic law and hence forbidden to marry. A (returned woman pilgrim) gave her opinion — that there was no bar to marriage — and there was general agreement that her decision must be right. The marriage ceremonies were completed two years later in the usual manner" (Tapper 1978: 382-383). Similar examples of women's ability to transpose a position of religious authority into one of secular power recur throughout the world. They provide women with considerable experience in decision-making and political management.

In an article on Mende women in Sierra Leone, Hoffer (1974) details an extraordinary woman's rise to political power and paramount chieftanship. Integral to Madam Yoko's creation and manipulation of political alliances was her use of girls' initiation societies. By sponsoring the initiations and circumcision of girls in the bundu bush (or sande), Madam Yoko also became the sponsor of their marriages. When the young women were brought out of the initiation ceremony, their parents permitted her to arrange their marriages, saying "'No, Madam, we have given these children to you; you are the owner of these girls. You may give them in marriage to anyone you please.' She gave them to husbands, to constables and noble men of the country" (Hoffer 1974: 182). In this way, she consolidated a farreaching political base by giving large numbers of initiated girls in marriage.

In Sierra Leone, arranging marriages was a well established way of cementing political alliances and a political strategy used widely by both men and women with political aspirations. Men, however, were limited in the number of women's marriages they could influence by the number of women with whom they shared kin-based interests; they were further limited in the number of wives they could accept to the number they could support. Madam Yoko, on the other hand, could make alliances in both directions in ever expanding numbers. She could accept girls 'in' to sponsor their initiations; then, after being their direct patron for only a short while, she could marry them 'out' to forge alliances throughout Sierra Leone. In addition, she could dispose of her own sexual favors, allying herself with men leaders directly, and had she not remained childless throughout her life, she would have bound her politically influential lovers and husbands to her through their mutual offspring. Ultimately, Madam Yoko "was recognized a paramount chief in 1884 by the British colonial government... paramount over all the Kpa Mende, ruling an area that, 13 years after her death in 1906, broke down into 14 separate chiefdoms" (Hoffer 1974: 176).

Madam Yoko is a particularly striking example of a traditional women's leader who turned informal ritual associations to her own political profit. Throughout the world, however, there are many such examples: individual women who base their personal social and political power on the female authority and solidarity legitimated by their involvement in traditional religious activities, even though those activities may themselves be seen from another perspective as being part of the system repressing women.

Although informal ritual and religious associations constitute one of the main avenues through which respectable women in traditional societies enter public life and learn political skills, female religious leadership does not necessarily promote the goals of its women constituents exclusively or even primarily. In many societies, women would have no significant, legitimate public voice without a ritual or religious forum, but such a voice will not always speak for all the women involved equitably. We do not know, for example, whether Madam Yoko was particularily responsive to women's needs; the solidarity she forged with other (mostly male) chiefs of comparable rank may well have overtaken any initial identification she had with the women from whose ritual associations she rose. Similarly, the returned pilgrims, shrine keepers, mullah-s, or any of the many women's religious leaders we have discussed may put the political skills they acquired in the women's informal associations to a variety of ends — to serve the interests of their lineage, household, class, local community, or themselves -- rather than to the collective ends of the female sodality itself or to meet the personal needs of its women members.

Even though women's informal ritual and religious associations do not exclusively uphold a male-defined status quo, not all active female religious leadership stands at the apex of a self-conscious female solidarity, nor are all women's leaders in themselves woman-oriented. Just as we questioned whether active economic associations redistributed or concentrated resources, so, too, we must ask whether authority in active ritual associations promotes the interests of all participants or privileges only a few.

AN AUTONOMOUS RELIGIOUS AUTHORITY?

Religious authority entails more than leadership. Its legitimacy derives not only from a constituency of citizen-followers, but from a constituency of believers who share a commitment to a system of ideas about the ultimate order of things. That order is never unproblematical nor is it transparently recreated in the real world, but its principles are the ones people consider in judging their world and the human relationships in it. We readily recognize the religious bases for many forms of men's political action in societies where 'church' and 'state' are not as rigorously separated as they have become in the west. We presume that the legitimacy of men's actions in such circumstances derives at least in part from a religious conception of male authority, from the rights and obligations of men as they reflect accepted supernaturally ordained gender ideals. We now need to ask whether religious and ritual conceptions of gender-linked legitimacy shape any consistent patterns of political authority among women.

A separate, parallel hierarchy of female leaders does not by itself guarantee that the legitimacy they attain in women's informal ritual and religious associations will uphold an autonomous or more egalitarian women's religious authority. There are, however, many instances in which women's religious authority stems not only from a parallel leadership, but, more importantly, from a separate female conception of the sacred world order: an autonomous women's authority that bases its legitimacy in a distinct women's concept of female power.

Spirit Possession and Shamanism. Spirit cults, which offer many opportunities for a politically important women's leadership, are a widespread example of women's ritual associations that invoke this separate conception of religious authority. Spirit cults tend to be of two primary sorts: (1) cults established around a particular spirit medium, who through trance is able to interpret the spirit world for clients and followers; and (2) more diffuse spirit possession which afflicts lay persons without intermediaries. In both kinds of possession, spirits or divinities legitimate human action. They may make their wishes known either by speaking directly through the mouths of the possessed individuals, or those wishes may be interpolated from other signs the supernatural provides. In either case, the netherworld makes demands upon this world, indicating the steps which must be taken to satisfy the divinities and to redress imbalances among humans which have disrupted relations with the spiritual world. Everywhere, women tend to be the key individuals in spirit cults, both as mediums and as client-victims.

As with formal ritual and religious associations among women, women's involvement in spirit cults is often interpreted as an essentially defensive strategy, a reaction to their exclusion from other sources of power. After summarizing many examples of spirit possession among women, Lewis concludes "that we are concerned here with a widespread use of spirit possession, by means of which women and other depressed categories exert mystical pressures upon their superiors in circumstances of deprivation and frustration when few other sanctions are available to them" (1966: 318). His point of view has been taken up in numerous other studies (Berger 1976; Fakhouri 1968; Freed and Freed 1967; Gomm 1975; Harper 1963; Lerch 1977; Lewis 1966, 1967, 1971, 1974; Morsy 1978 a and b; Morton 1972-3; Nathanson 1975; Nelson 1971; O'Nell and Selby 1968; Rubel 1964; Shack 1971; Young 1975). In most of these case studies, spirit possession occurs more frequently among 'women and other depressed categories.' It is interpreted as a distinctive style of "bargaining from weakness" (Gomm 1975) wherein the demands of people without secular authority can be given voice, in the name of the spirits, though the mouths of mediums or victims of possession. It is not seen, then, to be the spirits who truly speak, but the disenfranchised themselves.

But if, in this pursuit of "spiritual patrons" (Lerch 1977), spirit possession is at base a defensive strategy, it also organizes women's ability to respond assertively. The women who participate are not exclusively, in Berger's terms, "status seekers" who accept the definition of their social and religious position imposed by formal male religious society; they are also, according to Berger, in some sense "rebels" (1976). That is, they do not subscribe to the same definition of women's religious authority held by men, but hold a different view of legitimate female power.

Both Siegel (1978) and Holmberg (n.d.) have shown that women's association with spirit mediumship is not simply an attempt to obtain legitimation in men's eyes, or to obtain spiritual patronage powerful enough to counterbalance the women's powerlessness vis-a-vis men. The women's spirit mediumship described in Atjeh by Siegel is not an attempt on the part of women to force entry into the male domains of authority. Indeed, Siegel argues that men's and women's bases for authority are quite distinct. Men, in Atjehnese Sumatra derive their authority from the recitation of Islamic text: their authority is legitimated in the rational and measured words of those texts. Women, on the other hand, are not constrained by this sense of formal Islamic rationality. This does not mean, however, that they are irrational; their possession by <u>djinn</u> spirits is not irrational, but it "has authority which comes from a different source" (Siegel 1978: 21).

Men do not deny the existence of the djinn, but they will not agree with the women that djinns affect human life -- either in dreams or in illness. The women not only accept the djinns' influence on human experience, but women who become curers acknowledge a direct personal relation with the djinns. The curer, according to Siegel, must be willing "to let the bodiless djinns use her body as their 'voice.' ... Initially, the spirits chose her and occupied her body. Once she agreed to let them speak through her, however, they became her set of spirits whom she summons when she has need of them. ... What she agreed to in her compact with the djinns is to be their sounding box and set of props. She has escaped illness by converting their language into her speech" (1978: 28). To the men, language of the djinns, not being Koranic, must be false because only the fixed statements of the Koran are true. For the women, however, the Koran is an inadequate statement of "women's desires that are unfulfilled" (Siegel 1978: 24); the daily flux in women's lives is given expression in the language of the djinns. The men's vision of the world cannot quite deny the women's but the personal relation which women establish with the other-than-rational djinns stands in sharp contrast to the men's vision of the proper religious order.

Holmberg's study of Tamang religion in highland Nepal (n.d.) also explores the ways in which shamanism particularly expresses a female perspective. He shows how women and shamans, along with a divinity called <u>tsen</u>, all occupy structurally homologous positions in the social and religious order. In the social world, women live simultaneously in and between two different patriclans: they are born into one patriclan with which they maintain vital relations all their lives, but they move to join and forge equally important relations in their husbands' patriclans. Women are permanently torn between the two groups and actively mediate between them.

Tsen are an ambiguous kind of divinity. A tsen female was once married to a human being, but the husband's lack of respect for his wife's kin and their gifts to her precipitated a divorce. Their divorce marked the primordial separation of divinity and humanity. Today, tsen are known to humans as sprites of the midspace between heaven and earth. Tsen can also attach themselves to individual women and be inherited by one woman from another. A woman who has inherited one must worship her tsen respectfully: through her tsen either blessings or misfortune can come into her household, depending upon whether the tsen is kept satisfied or not. In this way, tsen mediate between the woman's household and the divine realms.

To worship tsen, the services of a shaman are needed. Shamans, like women, have personal tsen attached to them; like tsen and women, shamans are associated with the mediation of social groups as well as the mediation between human and divine. Holmberg shows, then, that all three -- women, shamans, and tsen -- share "a vision" of the social and religious order, which looks at the world from the vantage of one caught between its various parts, whether between intermarrying patriclans or between heaven and earth.

This alternate vantage, according to Holmberg, emerges not only in relation to women and their social experience, but also in counterpoint to the vantages expressed in other facets of the total Tamang religious system -- the lamaic and the chthonic. Holmberg demonstrates how the perspectives expressed in these other two aspects of Tamang religion emphasize determinacy, closure, and continuity. He shows how this emphasis draws upon the social experience of men in Tamang society, who do not move at marriage, but instead are part of locally continuous patrilines. Men experience women's double allegiance to natal and marital kin as disruptive and distracting. Lamaic and chthonic ritual attempts to deny the disruptive potential of marital exchanges and to establish a measured continuity in those exchanges.[2]

E. Ardener describes a similar tension between the male and female view of the spirit universe among the Bakweri in West Africa. There, women are afflicted by wild "mermaid" spirits called liengu. The liengu are associated with the wild uncontrollable universe beyond the village boundaries. Bakweri men live and work inside the village boundary fences and perceive everything which operates beyond those fences as threatening and uncontrollable. The women, who must go outside the fences every day for their livelihood, overlap with the domain of the liengu.

The women's association with liengu, however, appears to suggest very different meanings to men and to women. To men, women's possession by the liengu is dangerous; the liengu do not belong in the world of human life and so must be exorcised. Women do not share this view of the world order and hence interpret the association with liengu spirits as dangerous only if it is not properly acknowledged. "The male interpretation is that the liengu rites cure a spiritual illness. That is why male doctors take a spiritual part. The women nod at this sort of interpretation in male Bakweri company but there is a heady excitement when the liengu subject is raised in the absence of Bakweri men. It is accepted that the liengu mermaid spirits do 'trouble' the women, and cause them physical symptoms. The trouble is solved when a woman becomes a liengu" (E. Ardener 1972: 151). The liengu initiate is formally introduced into the adult women's interpretation of the world by a sponsor, or "liengu mother," and is taught all the rules applying to adult liengu womanhood. "Passage through liengu rites shows that a girl is a woman; her fellow-women vouch for it. The men feel a danger has been averted; she has been rescued from the wild and is fitted for marriage with men. But she still continues to bear a spirit name, and converses with fellow-women in the mermaid language" (E. Ardener 1972: 151-152).

---

[2]Holmberg also goes on to observe that, while each of these vantages —or visions -- reflects a view of the world taken from the perspective of one sex or the other, ultimately each is abstracted in the religious system in such a way that both gender-marked visions are meaningful to people of both sexes.

Both men and women believe in liengu spirits and acknowledge their disrupting potential. But men feel the solution lies in exorcising the spirits and keeping them at bay, while women disarm the liengu by domesticating them, by maintaining lifelong relations with them, and by bringing them into the web of human society.

The Women's War. These rituals, like the initiation rituals discussed earlier, promote female solidarity not only through the shared experience of the ritual procedures, or through the ascendancy of a female leadership, but also through their affirmation of an alternative female world view. While the women's reality affirms their special vulnerability with regard to their men, it also provides an organized avenue for consolidating an autonomous female response to male power.

The implications for women's political opportunities depend upon whether autonomous female religious legitimacy is vested only (or primarily) in the women's leadership, thereby creating another (albeit female) elite, or whether it devolves upon all women equally. Only when any woman can invoke the legitimacy of a separate female power — and when any woman's invocation of her femaleness implicates the solidary femaleness of all women — does an autonomous female religious authority effectively redistribute women's ritual power among all women. Universal or equitably distributed female religious authority must be rooted in a conception of uniform female solidarity.

One of the most striking demonstrations of such a solidary female power culminated in the "Women's War" or the "Aba Riots." Both terms refer to a women's revolt in southeastern Nigeria where, in 1929, "tens of thousands" of women rose up in arms against the British colonial administration (Van Allen 1976: 60). Since many excellent accounts of these events are available, we will use this uprising to illustrate the informal organizational bases for political action and to highlight the potential political impact of religio-cultural ideals of female solidarity.

The hostilities of the "Women's War" of 1929 grew from increasing imbalances in the economic positions of the sexes and were precipitated by a misunderstanding over taxation between British colonial agents and the women of southeastern Nigeria (Romalis 1979). Although men alone had been taxed since 1925, the communication networks of women's ritual and market associations began to promulgate rumors that, following the reenumeration census then underway, women, too, would be taxed. Skirmishes originated as individual women challenged the authority of British-appointed enumerators to count women and women's property. Ifeka-Moller cites one incident from the British reports:

> An over-zealous census enumerator, acting on behalf of one warrant chief, Okugo, of Oloko village in Owerri Province, became involved in an incident with a woman. This woman, Nwanyeruwa, who became the heroine of the women's war, alleged that on 23 November the enumerator:
>
>> came to her house whilst she was squeezing oil and asked her to count her goats, sheep and people. She replied angrily, concluding with the pointed question: 'Was your mother counted?' Thereupon Emeruwa (the enumerator) seized her by the throat and she, with her hands covered with oil, held him also by the throat, and raised the alarm (Report: 13).

Matters then escalated. Chief Okugo unwittingly transformed protest into revolt when he abused and assaulted women who had come to his house in order to protest about their supposed impending taxation (Ifeka-Moller 1975: 131).

Shortly thereafter, three localized riots broke out in Owerri Province, but soon there was widespread rebellion throughout both Owerri and Calabar Provinces, covering an area of 6,000 sq. mi. and inhabited by a population of some two million.

The women massed to attack prisons and courts, releasing inmates and destroying sixteen of the British 'native courts.' Eventually, the colonial administration called up military troops to put down the women's rebellion. The report of an English lieutenant, commanding some of the troops used against the women, described what struck the British most about the women's activities:

> Some were nearly naked wearing only wreaths of grass round their heads, waist and knees and some were wearing tails made of grass. The District Officer then began to talk to the crowd. Only a few could hear him owing to the noise the others were making. During all this time reinforcements of women were continuing to arrive both by river and land. Some of these were carrying machetes... During this time when I was not standing with the District Officer I moved up and down the fence (which marked off the administrative offices) telling the women not to make a noise. They took no notice and told me that I was the son of the pig and not of a woman ... The Court clerk and policeman were interpreting for me and told me the women, speaking in native language, were calling the soldiers pigs and were telling the soldiers that they knew they wouldn't fire but they didn't care whether the soldiers cut their throats (Minutes of Evidence by a Commission of Inquiry Appointed to Inquire into Certain Incidents at Opobo, Abak and Utu-Etim-Ekpo in December 1929, 1930: 7) (in Ifeka-Moller 1975: 129).

The troops did, however, fire on the assembled women on two occasions, killing more than fifty and injuring as many. It took four months for the uproar over the rumored census to settle down.

The British reports record the sequence of events not as a "War," as it is remembered by the Igbo and Ibibio women, but rather as "riots," conveying the impression of irrational and disorganized action,[3] rather than a concerted or strategic women's uprising. Although the revolt appeared spontaneous, outrageous, and excessive to British observers, it was, in fact, extremely well organized. Its organization just did not follow the lines of the formal political and jural machinery established by and familiar to the British. The women were organized informally. Although opinions differ about which was more important,[4] the women's rebellion drew its strength from two distinct sources. First, there was the

---

[3]The parallel here is apparent with the commonly presumed 'irrationality' of women's spirit possession.

[4]See especially Ifeka-Moller 1973 and 1976.

informal organizational tradition of women's ritual sodalities, market associations, and kinship-based political pressure groups; and, in addition, there was the women's shared sense of their femaleness with its concomittant cultural rights and religious authority.

We have already considered the political effectiveness of women's informal associations. The kin-based political groups of women, like the agbo or mikiri meetings of 'daughters of the lineage' and 'wives of the village,' the market associations headed by leaders like the iyalode, and the ritual associations like the bundu or the sande sponsoring girls'initiations were all important bases for women's political action. the relative importance of these different informal women's associations appears to have varied from one ethnic group to another in the 1929 Nigerian case, the importance of political organization remains the same. Informal associations such as these, although formed for differing purposes, organize groups of women to defend the rights and promote the interests of their participants. They act through the credibility of their leadership within the wider political systems and through the effectiveness of the communication networks they engender.

The women leaders of these kin-based, village, market or ritual associations served not only to link other women to the formal authority that they shared, as leaders, with their male counterparts. They could also invoke the unique strategies of aculturally and religiously defined female solidarity. Speaking of the girls' initiation societies in Sierra Leone, Hoffer writes that "there is pain and risk of death from infection [from the genital operations involved] in the initial ordeal in the Bundu grove. This shared experience helps to bond the initiates together into a cohesive group. They swear an oath in the Bundu bush never to reveal the fault of another Bundu woman" (1975: 158). The solidarity forged in the bundu initiation grove continues throughout the lives of the initiates:

> Within neighborhoods of larger provincial towns, Bundu women tend to stick together, giving each other advice and assistance. During holidays and the initiation season, groups of Bundu women go out through the streets of the town, singing their songs and dancing. To see a close-packed contingent of Bundu women dancing through the street, singing their exclusive songs, shaking their gourd rattles in time with their swaying, is to see a display of female solidarity. Even in Freetown, the only truly urban area in Sierra Leone, Bundu offers companionship, mutual help, and assistance in life crisis events which most women experience (Hoffer 1975: 161).

The solidarity of Bundu women and women in other similar female initiation sodalities goes far beyond a psycho-social defense against their special vulnerability as women or the ordeal of initiation. Bundu women, for example, exercise considerable collective power over men. Even the holders of high political offices are subject to bundu authority, as one case described by Hoffer clearly demonstrates:

> Paramount Chief Samuel Africanus Caulker, who ruled [in Kagboro Chiefdom] from 1919 to 1932, became an imperious old fellow, and used abusive language in talking to his wives. As the story is told, after an especially colorful outburst, an abused wife said: 'Excuse me, sir. Did you say...?' and she repeated the offending phrase.

'You are ...right,' he replied. The wife went away, but returned with the Bundu women in town. They physically carried the paramount chief away to the Bundu bush. When he came back, a (male) informant narrated, 'he was soooo mild' (1975: 161).

In addition to their right to judge offenses against their members and impose fines or other routine punishments upon the offenders, women's informal associations, like the ritual initiation societies described here, used tactics that identified the transgressions of the living not just as infractions of the everyday order of sexual and political rights but as abominations against the permanent sacred order of the world. Chief Samuel Africanus Caulker's abuse not only wronged his wife, but all women and all female ancestors. "Disrespect toward women not only offends the living, but also the ancestors, who are the ultimate source of all secret society law and all blessings" (Hoffer 1975: 155). Therefore, his offense not only disrupted his relations with his wife, but threatened the entire order of supernaturally ordained relations between men and women. The power of the women's associations in redressing such wrongs lay finally in the authority of legitimate female solidarity in that religious world order.

After the rebellious incidents of 1929, when the British colonial authorities learned of the existence of the women's networks, they began to recognize their role in the circulation of information and to witness the female solidarity that the networks engendered. But the British remained ignorant of the cultural, ideological, or religious bases for the women's activism. As Van Allen summarized:

> During the investigations that followed the Women's War, the British discovered the communication network that had been used to spread the rumor of taxation. But that did not lead them to inquire further into how it came to pass that Igbo women had engaged in concerted action under grassroots leadership, had agreed on demands, and had materialized by the thousands at Native Administration centers dressed and adorned in the same unusual way — all wearing short loincloths, all carrying sticks wreathed with palm fronds, and all having their faces smeared with charcoal or ashes and their heads bound with young ferns. Unbeknown to the British, this was the dress and adornment signifying "war," the being used to invoke the power of the female ancestors (Harris 1940: 143-145; 147-148; Perham 1937: 207ff; Meek 1957: ix) (1976: 73).

Because the British did not recognize the religious and ritual symbolism of the women's actions, they not only failed to see the system of beliefs about female power underlying the women's symbolic action, but also could not appreciate how such actions might, in a purely Igbo or Ibibio context, be quite effective. The palm fronds and ferns, nudity, obscenity, greenery, and filth used by women in the 1929 uprisings were not randomly chosen props for chaotic and disruptive behavior. They were part of the traditional women's political strategy, used by women's kin-based, village, market, and ritual associations alike, known as 'making war on a man' or 'sitting on a man.' 'Sitting on a man'

> involved gathering at his compound, sometimes late at night, dancing, singing scurrilous songs which detailed the women's

grievances against him and often called his manhood into question, banging on his hut with the pestles women used for pounding yams, and perhaps demolishing his hut or plastering it with mud and roughing him up a bit. A man might be sanctioned in this way for mistreating his wife, for violating the women's market rules, or for letting his cows eat the women's crops. The women would stay at his hut throughout the day, and late into the night, if necessary, until he repented and promised to mend his ways. Although this could hardly have been a pleasant experience for the offending man, it was considered legitimate and no man would consider intervening (Van Allen 1976: 168-169).

In 'sitting on a man,' women respond to an assault on their traditional rights as women with tactics emphasizing their solidarity as women and invoking the religious symbolism of female power.

Such behavior has been described by many ethnographers of the West African coast (Green 1964; Harris 1939-40; Ifeka-Moller 1973, 1975; Leith-Ross 1939; Van Allen 1972, 1976), but S. Ardener's (1977) and Ritzenthaler's (1960) accounts of the Kom anlu are probably the most complete. Anlu, according to Ritzenthaler, traditionally referred to a disciplinary technique employed by women for particular offenses. These include beating someone or uttering insulting obscenities like 'Your vagina is rotten'; beating a pregnant woman; committing incest; seizing a person's sex organs during a fight; getting or being a nursing woman pregnant within two years after the birth of a child; and abusing old women (1960: 151). The original offense, then, is typically committed against an individual woman, but the procedures of anlu reinterpret it as an insult against all women and against the symbolic place of femaleness in the sacred order of the world.

According to the various accounts, a woman who thinks she has been abused because of her femaleness ululates -- screams in a piercing, wavering, ritualized way. The women of her solidarity group — whether based on kinship, residential, market, or ritual associations -- are said to rush to her aide when they hear such a cry. They listen to her complaint, and if they agree that it was an attack upon her femaleness (and not because she was quarrelsome, or stingy, or some other feature of her person not unique to her gender as the Kom understand it), it becomes an assault upon their collective femaleness. They agree upon a date in the near future when they will reassemble to extract justice. On that date, they dress in vines, smear themselves with mud, and descend upon the offender (usually, but not always, a man). They sing obscene songs, plaster him with excrement, wreak havoc in his residential compound, generally humiliate him, and finally require him to admit to his guilt and pay fine to the women's sodality.

S. Ardener (1977) and Ritzenthaler (1960) recount in detail the 1958 anlu brought against one unfortunate man. Teacher Chia, it seems, had been among the promoters of contour plowing, which was being encouraged by the local agricultural extension agency and the Catholic church. He wanted to convince the Kom women agriculturalists to plant horizontally across the slopes of the hillsides, rather than working their furrows up and down the slopes as was their custom, "not", as S. Ardener observed, "you might think, a very provocative requirement" (1977: 38). Impetuous in his enthusiasm for reform, Teacher Chia not only established a demonstration farm, but also uprooted some of the women's crops which were not contour planted. To Kom women, Teacher Chia's efforts infringed on the traditional organization of agriculture in such a way that he compromised women's prerogatives as farmers, and, collectively, as females.

First, a couple of women spat in his face.

Then a third woman, Mamma Thecla Neng, doubled over and shrilled the 'Anlu' war cry, which was echoed and re-echoed in a widening circle beginning with the women who had been in attendance at the Council. Fright gripped Chia and he started for his bicycle only to find it covered with twines, around which a growing number of women were dancing and singing. Women started to pick up bits of stones to throw them at him cursing him as they did so. He ran to the Mission House and made for the Father's latrine. The Rev. Father bolted the door and stood with his back to it. The women gathered in dance, and vines and branches were cut and heaped in front of the latrine (F. Nkwain IN Ardener 1977: 36).

Then the women went out in full anlu. They withdrew to a nearby hillside to sing, dance, and put up their own 'demonstration farm' -- with, of course, vertical planting. Before the crisis was over, 2000 women left for the main city "wearing vines, and with unwashed bodies and painted black" (Ardener 1977: 39); another 4000 women -- older women and nursing mothers -- struck in sympathetic revolt in the local market.[5] Their actions convinced the police not to take reprisals against the rebelling women, nor to continue enforcing contour planting efforts.

For some time, those who opposed this anlu uprising were ostracized and prevented from attending public functions and ceremonies, funerals, childbirth feasts, and from cooperative farming. These were traditional anlu methods of forcing quick penitence. Eventually peace was made and things settled down, although to a new order. The women's anlu leader was given a seat on the local council. The Catholics and the anlu women became reconciled. Indeed they teamed up against the American Baptists who were said to have referred to the women as "anlu-nuts." Mr. Chia made his peace with the women too. He recalls the day when the women 'cleansed' both him and his compound: "I felt good after that," he is quoted as having said, adding that one should remember to "be careful with our mothers" (Ardener 1977: 40).

In her analysis of such events, S. Ardener underscores the importance of the underlying sense of female solidarity in these actions. This solidarity does not constitute a group or an association in the usual sense, but instead unites all women within the societies in question. Because women's solidarity in these cases derived from their shared femaleness, it crystallized into revolt when an offense was made against the traditional preserves and prerogatives of that femaleness. Those prerogatives in turn stemmed from fundamental domestic, economic, familial, and sexual rights and obligations of all women, regardless of the specifics of their personal situations. It is not surprising that the revolt itself activated important cultural symbols of femaleness qua femaleness. Once the women began to 'make war' or 'sit upon' an adversary, both

---

[5]Total Kom population was approximately 30,000.

offense and rebellion transcended the particularities of the situation from which they arose and were translated into a generalized offense against the collective legitimacy of all women. The result was a form of militant solidarity which evoked the local symbols of that femaleness.

Among the Igbo, Bakweri, and other such groups in West Africa, (and perhaps, as S. Ardener suggests, for groups of rebellious women in many parts of the world, including contemporary feminist action in the west), many of the most basic symbols of collective femaleness are sexual. Sexual insults and taunting appear to be particularly powerful in this context, not simply because they are taboo forms of feminine behavior, translate an assault against one woman or a demand made upon women in but because they unify all women against all outside threats. They specific contexts into a non-isolable offense against the basic shared femaleness of all women. Such offenses against women are not them-selves universal; they grow out of a particular cultural and religious view of the place of femaleness and women in the world. Among the Bakweri, E. Ardener, as we have seen, argues that women are associated conceptu-ally with the wild uncontrollable universe of 'nature' which exists outside the ordered rational life located within the villages. Femaleness, according to this perspective, is an untamed force conceived of as analogous to, or part of, other natural forces beyond the control of 'man.' According to E. Ardener, the Bakweri interpret this 'man' literally: that is, they associate predictable social life with men. This men's order is constantly threatened by women's continued associations outside of that order.

We might choose to interpret this women's 'outsideness' as an exclusion from the formal structures of communication, decision-making and power, and for Bakweri men, women's exclusion has double-edged symbolic meaning. Not only can women never be completely trusted within the social world, but they can threaten the very foundations of that world by bringing the chaos of the wild forest and sea into the heart of the fenced-in villages.

Such, however, is the precariousness of the men's order. E. Ardener suggests that Bakweri women hold quite another view. He examines women's ritual sodalities and maintains that women do not see the natural world as an affliction, but, rather as a structured and legitimate world into which they can be initiated and with which they maintain positive ties. Thus, to the extent that women are in active collusion with the natural order, the men's fears that the women might destroy the male social order are well founded. When the women wear palm fronds or vines, when they throw mud and excrement, when they mass and rebel, they are not simply going on a political and economic strike. They are invoking a universe over which the men acknowledge that they have no control.

PART THREE

Linkages to the Formal Sphere

6

Personal Connections

Our focus on the internal dynamics and semi-autonomy of informal associations has helped in identifying the economic and political power bases of people who are largely isolated from formal institutions. It underscores their productivity, ingenuity, and influence, which might not otherwise be as apparent. But the internal dynamics of such informal associations must also be understood in the wider context of their linkages with the formal sector, especially as we move from an analytical to an applied plane.

Expanding women's access to resources, information, skills, and power requires better integration of women into the formal institutions of their society. Hence, effective linkages between formal and informal organizations must be created. But informal associations are already connected with formal institutions in a variety of ways, and many of their strategies are in fact responses to these connections. Before creating new avenues of access, we ought to consider the kinds of linkages that are already in place and ask whether they warrant reinforcement or need neutralization.

Two principal types of connections call for analysis. Linkages can be personal, operating through individual informal leaders who act as cultural, political, or economic brokers and speak for their local constituency. Or informal associations may be institutionally tied with formal political and economic structures through their activities as organized groups. Institutional or group connections are particularly common among the most formalized informal associations, such as women's voluntary associations and philanthropies, which often have direct institutional access to party bureaucracies, corporate businesses, and the like. These different kinds of linkage suggest different practical applications.

LEADERSHIP IN DEFENSIVE NETWORKS

As visible links between formal and informal spheres, women's leaders who are recognized, but informal, present an attractive point for development intervention. Women's patrons, ritual healers, or religious functionaries can, it would seem, become brokers of information, facilitating access to goods and services for the individual women in their respective networks.

A focus on local, informal leadership is also appealing because it fits into participatory strategies for development that are geared toward providing basic human needs. Efforts to recruit local leadership for development seem to conform with a more client-centered approach to human services, reflecting a concern for decentralized programs, local initiative, and the 'personal touch.' Such informal leaders have figured increasingly in plans to extend medical services through paramedics, in efforts to appoint village 'monitors' for special radio broadcasts, and in some of the Catholic Church's social programs that revolve around parish priests. It stands to reason, then, that, as we begin to recognize the importance of informal associations among women, the question of mobilizing their leadership should arise.

There are important limits to the capacity of such a diffuse and frequently defensive leadership to mediate between outside agencies and their local constituencies, however. Clearly, no set formula can be established, and assessments of the problems and potential of local leadership are in any case best undertaken in the field by insightful project planners. What prior analysis can do, however, is to clarify an essentially intuitive task by outlining the structural limits to achieving integration of poorer women into development programs through informal leadership.

Midwives and Curers. At the most diffuse and informal end of the spectrum of women's networks for mutual aid we find the defensive networks of midwives and women curers. It is to these practitioners that women often turn for informal professional medical guidance and advice. We may be tempted to view indigenous midwives and healers as quasi-professionals, each at the center of a personal network of clients; but their consultational relationship differs substantially from the professional roles with which we are most familiar. The relation between the midwife or healer and her clientele is not contractual, but is framed in terms of interpersonal obligation and responsibility.

The non-contractual nature of this relationship is vital. If the clients in the networks of midwife and healer were able to predict their medical needs precisely, and if they could be confident that they would always have the wherewithal to meet those needs, they might well structure a more formal exchange of services and payments, as takes place with hospitals and doctors. But the clients of a traditional local midwife or curer do not have clear or reliable access to formal medical services, nor can they easily or always afford such services. The interpersonal bond between midwife/healer and client guarantees service.

But the non-contractual nature of the relationship stems not only from the fact that the midwife/healer is generally practitioner to the poor. The midwife or healer provides widely varying services, largely in times of unpredicted crisis for client families; such a wide range in both needs and services can be articulated more flexibly and responsively within a context defined by interpersonal obligation than it can under the terms of a specific contractual arrangement.

From this perspective, the common imputation of divine calling to midwifery and healing takes on a new light. It is essential to the woman healer that her professional calling be validated both in training or skill as well as in an unequivocal mandate for ungrudging service to her clients. Such a mandate often consists of divine election for the role of midwife or semi-sacred healer. Her divine call to service not only sanctions her physical participation in healing activities, which may demand greater mobility and immodesty than would be appropriate to typical feminine behavior (Paul and Paul 1975); it also places the midwife/healer under an incontrovertible imperative to provide service that is tailored to widely variable personal needs. Thus, in addition to the personal ties she establishes within the network of her work, it is also the sacred or semi-sacred obligations of her calling which behoove the midwife/healer to respond to her clients' requirements when and how they arise.

Comanche eagle doctors are excellent examples of this kind of practitioner. Their medical knowledge derives its power from their supernatural eagle patron. In his biographical study of Sanapia, a Comanche puhakut, or 'eagle doctor,' Jones states: "The doctor must also be always accessible. He (sic) cannot refuse anyone his services. Sanapia conceptualizes herself, in the role of eagle doctor, as the medium through which the Medicine operates. She 'possesses' Medicine only in this sense, and, once she has committed herself to the life of a puhakut, it is no longer her decision as to who may or may not benefit from a supernatural power acting through her which can alleviate human suffering" (1972: 28). Such a doctor, says Jones, "must never extol his own abilities and should also dissuade others from doing so," and "should never suggest that he could cure an individual but must wait for the individual to approach him" (1972: 29-30). Although eagle doctors should be paid for services rendered, they "do not state a price but must accept whatever is offered" (1972: 81). These practices, which may set the eagle doctor up for some underpayment, protect patients' rights to responsive, affordable service.

Similarly, speaking of the traditional midwife in Morocco, Dwyer indicates that "her work in this capacity is sympathetic, willing, and cheap. She does not ask a set fee; instead, she is given whatever the new mother can afford. Moreover, when a new mother is poor, the 'arifa ['midwife,' see below] is typically generous: her gifts often exceed the delivery fee" (1977: 57). In the Moroccan case, this idiom of service is not sanctioned by divine ordination, but rather by reference to the servant or slave origins of the midwife. The Moroccan midwife "calls even a poor woman lalla or lady, for example, thereby signaling that she is serving rather than assuming control" (1977: 57). Her role as midwife/healer is not purely contractual, but is explicitly cast in a unique idiom to reinforce the obligations for unselfish interpersonal service.

This is not to say that midwives or healers are not medically skillful and capable; within the limits of their resources, they are. These indigenous curers know many techniques and remedies which are, even in our scientific sense, effective. Skill resulting in successful cures or deliveries is remembered by the client community, which seeks the more skillful midwives and healers before others. For precisely these reasons, it becomes tempting to ask whether the role might not actually provide an avenue for health care development.

The idea of working with local midwives and healers is appealing because, as indigenous practitioners, they understand the specific medical problems of underdeveloped sectors of the populace. Moreover, because of their record of unstinting service, midwife/healers are generally well respected in their communities. Their association with the spirit universe or need to do things not normally acceptable for women (such as travel at night) may make them occasionally suspect. Nevertheless, they are the major figures in local systems of community-based health care.

Certainly, the model of the Chinese barefoot doctor suggests that the indigenous medical system need not remain forever outside of planned improvements for national health care systems. There is undoubtedly room for much two-directional learning, to and from both indigenous and western practitioners. But there are limits to the integration of local midwives into rationalized systems of health-care delivery. The local midwife/healer cannot simply be turned into a neighborhood paramedical and pharmaceutical agent within the planned expansion of a western medical organization system. This would transform her former role as community healer so much that she would cease to be the liaison into the informal medical sphere, which made working with her appear so attractive in the first place.

Instead of thinking of these midwives and healers as ill-trained and poorly-remunerated quasi-doctors who need only more scientific training in order to bring the medicine of their communities into the twentieth century, we must learn to respect, not only their herbs, but also their position within the informal associational network of their clientele. We must also recognize that the informal web of personal ties and obligations which binds the midwife/healer to her patient/clients is not simply less or non-structured, compared to the organization of hospitals, doctors and formal medical care; rather, it is structured by the obligations of kin, community, friendship, and femaleness so as to serve especially vulnerable people. If these women are to lead efforts to improve women's health care, their relative autonomy and the legitimacy of their constituency must be preserved. More centralized health-delivery systems cannot subsume or fully rationalize the midwife's role, if they expect to derive continuing benefits from traditional practitioners.

Bridging the gap: the Moroccan 'arifa:[1]. Some informal leaders are able to represent their followers at the formal level. Such women commonly carry out this liaison task when appointed as, say, court or local government officials, where their customary arbitrational or representative roles may win limited formal recognition. Access to formal institutions may enhance the power of leadership, but its legitimacy usually remains rooted in the non-contractual compact between leader and community. For all the potential they appear to present as agents for development or brokers for cultural transformation, their mediating role remains limited by their informal commitments to their followers -- and by the overall relations between the women's informal sphere and the men's formal world.

The Moroccan 'arifa is one such example. The 'arifa is "the only woman employed by local Moroccan governments as a court official. She serves as an important liaison between the court and her district's women, and she operates in a variety of contexts in which contact between men and women must take place" (Dwyer 1977: 48). In her formal legal aspect, she is essentially an intermediary, a police chaperone whose sex puts her in a position to interpret Moroccan law for women. But the 'arifa is also the traditional informal midwife whose gynecological knowledge allows her to mediate some aspects of women's claims under the law.

Some of these intercessions occur at simple junctures between the midwife's medical expertise and societal legal concerns: thus, because it

_____

[1]Taken from the title of Dwyer's (1977) article.

is the 'arifa as midwife who verifies the bride's (family's) claims to premarital virginity, and because those claims are important not only to family honor but to the validity of the marriage, the legal testimony of the 'arifa as court official is essential in validating the legitimacy of marriages. But, as Dwyer points out, even at this simple level of feminine involvement in legal matters, the 'arifa has significant latitude for interpretation:

> In cases involving pregnancy and virginity testing, the 'arifa is said to make her assertations with women's futures in mind. Thus in one region in the south of Morocco, the 'arifa was credited with falsifying reports of virginity on several occasions. This option is always available to the 'arifa, it should be noted, for she tradition-ally has the right to slit the unperforated hymen of a young bride if consummation is difficult. With a judicious cut of the razor, the 'arifa thus can simulate virginal blood in a non-virginal bride. Similarly, with a judicious guess at the advancement of a pregnancy, the legitimacy of an illegitimate child can be established (1977: 63).

Because of the respect and deference accorded to an important 'arifa, she is apparently able to bend the truth under the law.

According to Dwyer, the 'arifa's role extends into more complex issues as well. The Moroccan 'arifa mediates directly between the system of police, courts, and prisons and the respectable women of the com-munity in several other ways. Should the police need to search a house, for example, the 'arifa precedes them into the women's quarters of the house, explains the police action to the women, and oversees the protection of the women's honor and modesty during the police intrusion. Moreover, women involved in marital or legal disputes with their husbands flee to, or are sent to, the house of the 'arifa for protective custody until the dispute is resolved. In all these cases, the 'arifa acts as an intermediary between the informal private world of women and the public formal one of men.

At her own discretion she may choose, at times, to act as an advocate and defender of women through adroit presentation of evidence. Her ability to intervene arises from her respected position within the defensive alliances of Moroccan women's sex-segregated world; but she also achieves her latitude for quasi-feminist activism because of her right to interpret the women's informal world to the men's formal judiciary. "[T]he 'arifa provides the judge with a combination of the woman's testimony, or corroboratory evidence as provided by witnesses, and of her own firsthand observations. She, in sum, submits a report in which the woman's point of view is more fully provided" (Dwyer 1977: 62).

In some ways this kind of interstitial position seems ideal for the mediation of development projects. The 'arifa, like analogous intermedi-ary women's leaders, is a spokeswoman for women's own interests who also has some influence in the formal judicial sphere. Because such women have been recommended for leadership roles in women's education, family planning projects, information campaigns, and so on, it is worth emphasizing the limits to their leadership in planned change originating from outside formal spheres.

Women's representatives like the 'arifa indeed often succeed in transforming women's defensive strategies into activist ones. But the activism of the 'arifa is constrained by the ultimate dependence of women's informal spheres on men's formal rights over women (in Morocco in this case). In any society, the opinions and interpretations of even the most outspoken 'arifa-like advocates for women's rights must be squarely framed within acceptable, male-defined limits: "In all of (her) duties, the 'arifa deals with the sexual aspects of womanhood. She protects and regulates female sexuality, but always with respect to male interests and prerogatives" (Dwyer 1977: 59). Because the men have recognized the 'arifa as their intermediary, they must accept her judgments, even though their ignorance of what transpires within the women's world admits the possibility of limited feminine conspiracy. But intermediaries like the 'arifa cannot defend women (such as prostitutes) whose deportment defies the limits defined by the prevailing social order.

Although even the most informal of women's associational networks within kindred, neighborhood, or community frequently have spokes-women, and although these individuals may be relatively outspoken at times, their license may be nevertheless limited by the wider societal subordination of the women's informal to the men's formal spheres. Such women's advocates remain bound, if not in their own behavior, then at least in their evaluation of other women's behavior, by the conventions of feminine propriety.

The potential of interstitial women as change agents is further limited because the balance they maintain between their support base and formal systems of authority is so delicate. If these leaders are to serve as effective mediators, the roots of their local legitimacy must be preserved at the same time as their institutional ties to outside authority grow strong. Ironically, though, the interaction of leaders like the 'arifa, midwives, or curers with formal institutions is closely restricted by their operational style, which follows the organizational rules of informal associations: they are bound to the other women in their professional networks by personal ties, cast in an idiom of obligation for flexible and unstinting service, mutual respect, and a shared understanding of women's vulnerability. Their leadership is an integral part of the organization of women's informal associations for their mutual defense. It may operate at the interface between formal and informal, but cannot itself be considered formal. Nor can it be formalized without seriously damaging the very relationships which give it its unique strength.

As an integrative strategy, then, efforts to make use of linkages through existing intermediaries cannot be altered to exceed the bounds set by the relationship between leaders and followers. First, when the constituency of an informal leader coheres around patronage and defer-ence, or sexual subordination, as the 'arifa's does, it operates only within clear limits to promote women's access to key parts of the labor force, public life, or other material benefits. Second, when a leader's contract with an otherwise remote outside authority begins to overshadow her personal, local commitments in the eyes of her followers, her credibility and recognition are likely to erode, and hence her capacity to mediate shrinks. Defensive networks are difficult to reach because they are by their nature covert. This is not to say that they operate outside of the so-called 'public' domain of their own communities, but rather to emphasize that participants usually perceive themselves as vulnerable in one way or another and are unlikely to submit to open recognition or scrutiny by institutions that touch their lives, as they see it, in primarily adverse or adversarial ways.

LEADERSHIP IN ACTIVE ASSOCIATIONS

By contrast, where informal leaders operate as women's public representatives and have embarked on active rather than purely defensive strategies, the possibilities for increasing their formal responsibilities may be greater. These leaders have, through their public activism, attained a greater measure of formal recognition, and the basis of their local support is less fragile since it has already been somewhat routinized through its activities. As leaders of active rather than protective associations, they can openly press claims or contest restrictions, albeit still within social limits. They can marshall some of the machinery of the formal system directly, as part of their accepted leadership role, whereas women who minister to exclusively defensive networks must revert to strategies that are indirect or covert.

It is chiefly in cases where formal authority already manifests a high degree of local legitimacy that informal leaders can emerge as brokers without jeopardizing their support base. One reason that westerners project considerable faith in the integrative capacity of local leadership may stem from our habitual view of formal authority as having a high degree of local legitimacy. Even those who accept a conflict model to describe government in western democracies assume a high degree of articulation, if not agreement, between formal and informal spheres. Similarly, in pristine simple political systems, where power is diffuse and informal associations are not sharply differentiated from formal ones, political leaders can stand simultaneously as representatives of both formal authority and their informal constituency with no apparent role conflict. Such was the precolonial position of the Lovedu Rain Queen for example (Krige and Krige 1943).

On the other hand, in systems where formal authority lacks full legitimacy or ramifying power in the eyes of local people, efforts to enlist informal leaders as agents of formal institutions have been most disruptive. In many peasant societies, where few channels to formal authority function systematically, the imperfect articulation between formal and informal spheres means that even the most active networks have an important covert component. To put it bluntly, leaders in even the most active informal associations have a limited capacity for mediation with formal institutions when those institutions are not fully trusted. Yet these are the very situations where indirect integration through informal leaders is often recommended.

A striking illustration of this point comes from Hutson's study (1971) of solidarity and individualism in a Swiss village, which indicates that the gap between the formal center and the largely informal periphery is not just a phenomenon of the women's sphere or the third world. When a would-be economic broker, the popularly elected village mayor, sought to introduce outside capital for land development, he met with local wariness and finally lost his position. His mandate as mayor, though formalized, rested largely on a commitment to represent the collective village interest. To the villagers, his activities on behalf of outside developers appeared to overstep his authority because, in their eyes, it violated his representative obligations and hence his local legitimacy. Subsequent development took place on a small scale, "initiated," Hutson writes,

> by a number of informal entrepreneurial leaders operating as agents in land sales made by individual villagers. The relation between agent and villager is a moral contract based on accepted values of equality and mutual aid, and the local entrepreneur takes pains to show that he is taking his commission out of the pocket of his outside-customer rather than of his co-villager-client (Hutson 1971: 94).

The greater visibility of leaders of active informal associations has masked these limitations on their leadership. These limitations become plain if we consider how the occasional efforts to recruit such leaders have torn at the very foundations of their representative vitality. Numerous examples in the colonial record dramatize the primary commitment of informal or semi-formal leaders to equality, mutual aid, and a kind of interdependent complicity with their associates, who legitimate the authority of those leaders more than superordinate powers can.

Some of the same structural limitations and contradictions that impaired colonial efforts at control may also hamper current attempts at development through informal leadership. In much of Africa and in parts of the Eastern Mediterranean, British rulers strove to limit social disruption by allowing only gradual development and the minimally necessary accommodation to change. In order to do so, they sought to rule indirectly through existing chiefs or village headmen. Ironically, because they were imposing a new stratum of overarching authority, they ultimately eroded the local support and legitimacy of these leaders. Particularly in the case of informal, popularly selected headmen, colonial administrators often thwarted their own goals because the introduction of formal requirements and recognition undermined popular support for traditional leadership. As the headmen came to be seen as agents of an authority to which villagers or tribesmen had few connections or loyalties, they ceased to have great influence at home (Taqqu 1977).

The history of the West African iyalode under colonial rule has parallels. The iyalode was a traditional office for the woman designated as the political leader and public representative of Yoruba women by colonial authorities; she was a chief in her own right, and thus part of the British policy of indirect rule. But the dilution of her power must be attributed not just to the already mentioned failings of that policy, but primarily to the fact that colonial administrators -- and their contemporary successors -- have "tended to relegate women to the background in their government" (Awe 1977: 146).[2] Colonial powers not only formalized

---

[2]Although such female chiefs were occasionally in a complementary position to male chiefs, there were great variations by region and over time; in general, because the iyalode was the only woman in the "crucial decision-making body", her power could easily be made subordinate to that of the male rulers (Awe 1977).

her position; because of their own preconceptions about the proper place of her sex in formal government, they intentionally diminished it.

Still, the simple introduction of extraneous formal regulations, definitions and routines were also an important factor in undermining local support. As Awe has emphasized in her study, the iyalode's original legitimacy and power derived fundamentally from her popular local support. Popular public approval gave her both authority among women and access to power and authority within the state, in her role as representative for all women. She maintained this support, moreover, through constant personal consultations with her networks of women to establish consensus on women's stands. In return, she received customary tributes and gifts as a sign of her continuing legitimacy in the eyes of her constituents. Under colonial domination, however, the iyalode lost much of her representative function as her relationship with formal authority became more rigidly defined. Since then, too, Awe writes, the customary gifts of her supporters have been replaced by a money salary from above (and one that compares unfavorably with that of her male counterpart). Both by subsuming her authority under theirs and by belittling her authority in relation to men's, colonial powers stripped the iyalode of legitimacy and power.

In contrast to Awe's account, Okonjo (1976) has written more optimistically about the partial revival of the traditional Igbo dual-sex political system, in which women leaders not unlike the traditional iyalode ruled women with an authority analogous to that of men leaders in parallel men's institutions. Okonjo suggests that at least one omu — the customary 'queen of women' in Nigerian Igbo communities -- has assumed both representative and mediating functions, and has actually spearheaded some successful self-help projects among the women she leads and represents. Traditionally, the omu's position corresponded to that of the male obi: both were crowned and acknowledged monarchs with parallel cabinets and chains of authority. The omu had responsibility for the women, and the obi for the men. Following a period of decline similar to that of the iyalode under colonial rule, the institution has re-emerged since Nigerian independence. This revival does not signal a complete return to a dual-sex system of political organization, however, for women reportedly continue to be excluded from government at the national level.

According to Okonjo, the town of Ogwashi-uku installed a new omu in 1972, who has since then established a working relationship with the local government and who simultaneously maintains a high social position in her community. She heads a cabinet, fixes the prices of agricultural goods, and can call policemen to her aid for enforcing the rules of the marketplace. Her role as liaison is thus more formalized and explicitly active than that of the Moroccan 'arifa, but at the same time her authority continues to rest largely on community loyalty and support. It is interesting, for example, that the omu and her cabinet still invoke supernatural remedies, performing market medicines designed to guard against disruption of the market. Despite her Christianity, her position thus continues to be "quasi-spiritual," in Okonjo's words, and it is more to match her capacity as a ritual or religious authority than as a representative of formal political authority that the idiom of her legitimacy is cast.

Nonetheless, from these multiple bases, the omu and her cabinet have instituted self-help activities in Ogwashi-uku, including the establishment of weaving cooperatives and the improvement of market stalls. Although Okonjo does not go into sufficient detail about the organization and achievements of these activities to allow much extrapolation, it is possible to guess at some of the reasons why these efforts have succeeded where others have failed. First and most obviously, her leadership is clearly of what we have called the active variety (although its defensive aspect should not be overlooked). More important, the organizational initiative here is voluntary. It is not only completely compatible with customary relationships, but is actually based on them. The government's main contribution has been its cooperative but non-directive stance, including and especially its acceptance of the omu's authority in the marketplace.

COMMUNICATION AS CHANGE

Beyond the basic need to maintain the local legitimacy of informal leaders, it is also useful to examine the extent to which information can be transmitted via informal leadership. Developmental change proceeds not just through the introduction of new resources, but equally through the transfer of new knowledge and skills. Scores of anecdotes and reports suggest that informal leaders may be good channels for the circulation of information under certain conditions, even when the introduction of material support through those leaders remains, as we have discussed, problematic.

The recognition of an informal leader's influence over the flow of communication has inspired two distinct strategies in development planning. First, 'opinion leaders' have been located and specifically recruited to bridge the communication gap with the outside agencies and to facilitate communication flow within their own localities. In the past, male leaders have been almost exclusively designated for such liaison roles, although a few recent projects have also attempted to recruit leading women. Selected individuals may, for instance, get special training and then be expected to help mediate change at the local level (Rahim 1976), whether as actual instructors (of, say, agricultural techniques, or principles of nutrition) or simply through the force of their example.

There are two major difficulties to bear in mind about communication strategies like these. On the one hand, the very local relationships upon which the effectiveness of the opinion leaders was based may be altered if the change agency assumes too active a role. When informal leaders begin to provide increased linkage with outside services and information, they may be perceived (and may identify themselves) more as part of the development bureaucracy than as part of their home communities and thus lose their local credibility. While such a goal may actually be suitable in a limited number of very dynamic contexts, in general such reactions obstruct the free flow of communication.

On the other hand, when information travels through intermediaries, it may easily be altered by the key individuals who act as a conduit. Opinions may be bent in unpredictable ways, and this is precisely why many projects have expressly rejected a leadership role for certain local notables. Many family planning projects, for instance, have explicitly denied local midwives a special role for fear of negative influence

(Hussein 1973). In other cases, women from elite families have been deliberately excluded out of a fear of their conservatism.

A second diffusion strategy, which avoids some of these difficulties, entails the identification and inclusion of local opinion leaders without, however, recruiting such women as the sole liaison with outside agencies. Hussein, for example (1965: 14), writes of a village family-planning campaign in Egypt that mandated special visits by social workers to leading families and also to traditional midwives in the hope that providing information to these key women would help set better informed community opinions. In Korea, where Mothers' Clubs have been established to disseminate contraceptive information and supplies and to aid in village development efforts, the participation of local opinion leaders was not planned from the outset, but has apparently carried considerable weight. A comparison of effective and ineffective clubs in two villages strongly suggests that success has hinged to a large degree on the participation of women with the greatest number of network linkages with other women and with connections to other cliques in their village (Rogers, et al. 1976). In this case, a woman's influence was not measured in terms of her occupation or social standing, but simply in terms of the number and concentration of her network ties, regardless of their actual content.

In order to avoid distortions in the social position of informal leaders on one hand and the conversion of valuable information into a scarce resource on the other, knowledge diffusion strategies should be as broadly based as possible. Informal leaders undoubtedly play important roles in shaping public opinion and in most cases should be included for this reason. Instead of singling them out as the primary linkage points, however, we might be better advised to include them within broader efforts at diffusion. Visits by agricultural extension agents, or other field workers, can be made not just to such leaders alone, but can be designed to draw in large numbers of other women as well. Large, open discussion forums between field workers and assembled villagers is one other technique that has been advocated and such methods can also extend to women in certain settings. Their advantage is that they include leaders together with a broad range of other village women.

Finally, when recruitment of selected women for special training does appear useful, the evidence suggests that known or established informal leaders might not always represent the best choice. Deciding precisely who should be considered as informal leaders should, at the very least, not hinge simply on socio-economic or occupational status but should also take social interconnectedness into account as an additional criterion. Occasionally, as in McCarthy's study of the recruitment of Bengali village women into the women's program of the Academy for Rural Development, informal leaders may be excluded altogether. In McCarthy's case study, it was not socio-economic leaders but rather marginal women — with respect to marital status or socio-economic standing -- who were in a position to respond to recruitment efforts. Yet, as teachers and organizers in their villages, they did make some slow headway, but "only as [they] exhibited direct, tangible profit from their work. That is, most of them began the second half of their roles as mediators, i.e. village demonstrations and instruction, by working quietly in their own [fields], making gardens, raising a few chickens, saving money, and gradually getting more food, acquiring livestock, and purchasing clothes. Such direct observable shifts in the economic conditions of the mediators paved the way for their acceptance and welcome in other [fields]" (McCarthy 1977: 368).

The problems of self interest on one hand and the fragility of relationships on the other become particularly salient when we turn our attention from communication to the related issue of material support. If an informal leader's access to information can sometimes skew her followers' perceptions of her role, so too any enhancement of her disposition over goods also stands to disrupt the moral covenant that underlies her position. In egalitarian associations, informal leaders can provide access to equipment, supplies, credit, or capital only if they appear loyal to the principles of equality, personal obligation, and mutual assistance. They must, in short, continue to observe their tacit compact with other women, somewhat after the fashion of Hutson's Swiss village entrepreneurs, or forfeit their influence. While this is not impossible it is no mean feat. If successful, it runs the second risk of encouraging inequality behind the veil of an egalitarian idiom. There are many examples in the development literature about informal leaders who simply appropriated funds or goods that were intended for wider distribution (see especially Staudt 1977). In asymmetrical associations such as patron-client groupings, increasing the flow of goods can all too easily exacerbate inequalities, perpetuating self interests that are ultimately inimical to the goals of development.

PLANNING CHANGE THROUGH INFORMAL LEADERS

To recapitulate, then, women who lead informal groups or who stand at the intersection of dense networks have an explicit but restricted role to play as mediators in development schemes. As links to build upon, they are limited not only because they are sometimes privileged people in pursuit of their own interests, but, more fundamentally, because of the conflicting demands of their interstitial position. The structural connections they provide between formal and informal spheres are appealing because they are both durable and elastic, but the balance they maintain is usually too delicate to sustain great transformation. Their limitations and potential as mediators of change can be summarized as follows.

Women who are central figures in the most defensive and vulnerable networks cannot easily be recruited as change agents. Most of them are limited by the ultimate derivation of women's informal sphere from men's formal rights over women. Nor is their implicit covenant with other women to provide mutual assistance and maintain equality compatible with the assumption of extensive contractual responsibility — particularly in settings where the authority that underwrites such contracts is perceived as unfriendly.

Among informal leaders we can distinguish a continuum of sorts that corresponds either to variations in the structure of their association or to nuances in the degree of formal recognition they have won. Generally, the more active the leadership, the more easily it can handle important roles in expanding formal institutions that are designed to stimulate development — from health-care systems to marketing organizations. There is considerable room for two-way learning and exchange between indigenous and more formalized structures; selected women healers, midwives or informal arbitrators may indeed be pivotal in encouraging such a two-directional flow. But, in most of the developing world, even the most active and semi-formalized leaders are restricted in their capacity as brokers by their ultimate allegiance to a code of local behavior that resists formalization. For best effect, then, the elaboration of formal, development-oriented institutions should not aim to subsume informal associations and leadership. The establishment of linkages that can accommodate the distinct organizational rules of informal associations is usually a better strategy; it is also one more capable of respecting local initiative and autonomy.

Communication networks provide one such linkage; and informal leadership can play a useful and even necessary role in conveying information between change agencies and local communities. How leaders are recruited or included will vary from case to case and is itself the subject of a separate field of study — one which properly ought to extend more systematically to the whole of women's worlds, and not just to issues of family planning (as it has to date). While leaders can be highly instrumental in the diffusion of information, much of the communications literature also suggests that efforts to make use of communication networks should not focus too narrowly on existing opinion leaders as identified only by socio-economic criteria. Especially in cases where resistance is expected, broadly based multi-level approaches may be more desirable.

By contrast, evidence cautions against the designation of informal leaders as established middlemen (sic) for the distribution of material goods. It is one thing to recognize women's borrowing and lending networks and then to encourage, say, a seed and fertilizer distribution scheme that takes such patterns of exchange into account. It is a different matter, however, to appoint one influential woman as gate-keeper to new goods, in the expectation that her informal mediating function will serve well here. This is not to deny the need for training women to be managers, bankers, local-level planners, professionals and para-professionals of all kinds. But it does point to the inadvisability of designing planning programs too specifically around informal leadership. The transfer of informal leadership functions to a formal organizational table is rarely straightforward and often impossible.

7

Institutional Linkages
and Group Organization
for Development

FORMALIZING INFORMAL ASSOCIATIONS

A second set of strategies for reaching women in the informal arena advocates the organizational transformation of women's informal associations into voluntary, local-level groups. · By building directly on existing associations, such transformations can reinforce institutional linkages between the formal and informal sectors. Only secondarily do they capitalize on links through individuals. The process tends to be based on group activities which give participants institutional, rather than personal, access to such formal organizations as established markets, banks, and courts or other government agencies.

Voluntary associations launched for development purposes may be large, as in the cases of women's clubs, neighborhood associations, or workers' organizations; or they may be designed on a deliberately smaller scale. The range of self-help projects in this category includes income-generating programs, the encouragement of work brigades, cooperatives or marketing organizations, and the creation of village radio-listening circles. Once voluntary associations are established, it should be possible, through organization at higher levels, to link them to one another, and even to a central change agency or a national government.

As a method for reaching informal associations and utilizing their strengths, this policy has been formulated to reinforce institutional linkages that are more systematic, predictable, and stable than connections through individuals. But it essentially calls for transforming the informal association into a formal organization. Just as the routinization of an informal leader's role can place her local legitimacy in jeopardy, the formalization of informal associations as groups similarly alters their internal dynamics and can undermine mutual trust and flexibility among members.

Confronting the Contradictions

If we consider our own cultural situation for a moment, this contradiction becomes apparent. This is the reason that we warn one another against buying a used car from a friend, taking a job with an uncle, or negotiating a loan from a close neighbor. In such instances, anxiety stems not only from fear that the transaction may fail, but from the more basic risk that primary, informal, and personal ties may be broken by the superimposition of secondary, impersonal, and contractual obligations.

On the other hand, primary and supposedly secondary (or contractual) ties coexist all the time within a variety of personal relationships. They need not be incompatible, as long as they are perceived as congruent. That is, the informal relationship must itself be disposed to assuming formal, impersonal commitments; and the formal obligation must be considered mutually acceptable by participants. Successful formalization of an entire informal association depends on the same two criteria.

The likelihood that informal relationships will accommodate the superimposition of new role expectations and obligations hinges on qualities such as the visibility and widespread social recognition of the association. Clandestine or illicit relationships, or defensive social networks that have been established to protect vulnerability, will almost certainly resist formal responsibilities. Such associations represent circumventions of formal authority, and the chances are slim that they may serve as bases for organizations sanctioned by that same authority. By contrast, highly visible and widely recognized relationships — such as mutual labor obligations, family ties among powerful classes, and certain types of patron-client ties — may more readily tolerate a second layer of formal rights and duties.

The acceptability of the formal organization in turn depends on such conditions as the perceived compatibility and accessibility of the new formal organization to members, the desirability of its purposes, the familiarity of new personnel associated with it, and the correspondence between its scale or internal differentiation and customary patterns of informal association. This requires that formal voluntary associations for development be organized to reflect and reinforce informal associational strengths.

Thus, efforts to organize loose clusters of interconnected women into large-scale, highly planned, and hierarchically structured groups run the greatest risk of failure on both of these counts; they almost certainly will undermine the informal associational vitality on which they depend. Safa, for example, shows how public housing in Latin America has destroyed the cohesion built up over many years in shantytowns, without any tangible compensation. Mutual aid is weakened in the planned community, and families become more suspicious of one another as the housing management begins to intervene in the internal affairs of the family. "The public housing family is alienated," Safa writes, "not only because of its low socio-economic status, which it shares with the shantytown, but because family and community life has been disrupted by the agencies of the state" (1976: 80).

On the other hand, the greatest chance for organizing formal voluntary associations for change from an informal base lies in combining (1) informal base associations that are already relatively active, bounded, and purposive from the outset with (2) intermediate levels of organization. In this way, we acknowledge the conflicting aspects of formal and informal organizations, presuming neither that the two are universally congruent nor that informal associations can readily be subsumed. By selecting the most active and most highly structured of informal associations as the ones which can best sustain formalization, we recognize that diffuse or defensive networks cannot be formalized. Similarly, the notion of intermediate levels of organization implicitly admits that not all formal organizations may be perceived by participants as acceptable.

1) <u>Active Associations</u>. Brana-Shute (1976) has discussed a case where Creole women in a lower-class neighborhood in Paramaribo, Surinam, became the effective core group of a local-level cell within a national political party. Ultimately, they became the brokers between neighborhood and national party headquarters, leading their party to local victory in the elections. Because the recruitment and organization of women into local coalitions or political pressure groups has often been advocated, and because organization in this case was at an intermediate level, these findings are relevant and intriguing.

In the Paramaribo neighborhood, women's political activism and influence grew initially out of their informal relationships and active solidarity. Women's clubs are fairly common among Creole women in Surinam, and are based on cohesive informal relationships of kinship, residence, and the sexual division of labor. Within the clubs, moreover, "'cores' of friends form work and communication units that increase the flexibility and influence of the club and allow members access to services and resources unavailable to them as individuals" (Brana-Shute 1976: 157). Internal initiative and the habit of active assertion were thus the driving forces for political organization. It is doubtful whether outside agents could have launched such a local movement. Political organization -- and ultimate electoral victory -- also resulted from the fact that women's network ties had assumed a corporate shape. It was the formal social club that actively adopted the political functions of a dormant party cell, and not the local cell that recruited the informally organized women (see also Chaney 1973; Hollander 1973; Jaquette 1973; Little 1972).

Active assertiveness in women's informal associations is closely related to such attributes as purposiveness and the presence of well defined group boundaries. Active informal associations tend to have specific purposes, although their objectives may shift. When these purposes are publicly stated and specialized, and when members tend to relate with one another primarily in terms of those purposes, the association can come to approximate formal organizations in several respects. Marketing cooperatives, political coalitions, or rotating credit associations, to name a few, are all relatively bounded informal groups with specific, stated purposes. Although still informal, they may organize themselves around a recognized nucleus and adopt varying degrees of internal differentiation and hierarchy. If their purpose becomes a formal criterion for membership, then the association actually comes to constitute a bounded group rather than a network alone. In this capacity, it may lend itself more readily to formalization.

Of course, active associations exhibit a full range of structures and purposes and only the most structured and purposive become the actual nuclei of formal self-help groups. The many examples of women's self-help development efforts that grew spontaneously out of traditional types of active solidarity have tended to involve groups that were highly bounded to begin with. Such associations had at the outset achieved a corporate group structure, had become coalitions or cliques, or were organized within carefully structured networks following principles of balanced reciprocity.

This point emerges repeatedly in Wipper's collection of papers about African women in rural development. In Mitero, Kenya, women have launched effective self-help groups, successors to the women's organizations, or ndundu, of earlier times, which draw on traditional patterns of association. The ndundu were not ad hoc meetings, but highly structured organizations with well-defined economic, social, and judicial functions. Membership was compulsory and included all the women who married into the lineage. In Nakuru, Kenya, by contrast, women's rural development organizations have been less successful. Although they too have based themselves on traditional associations -- such as informal market ties, an informal dance association, diffuse support networks and work groups --all these were too loosely connected to generate stable new organizations or experienced leadership (Wipper 1975-76).

Among the more structured groupings that can be mobilized into formalized self-help groups, we have earmarked rotating labor and rotating credit associations for special attention. Their relative boundedness and internal reciprocity may make it possible to establish formal ties with these associations without undermining their inner cohesion. Resources introduced into them may not simply ameliorate conditions temporarily but may contribute to a more self-sustaining cycle of improvement.

It is surprising that attention has lately turned away from both rotating credit and labor associations in favor of a more single-mindedly western model of cooperative action. To be sure, the principles behind cooperative movements are to protect the interests of all participants and engage all equally. Nevertheless, they are based upon a rationalist western model of political decision making, which is not uniformly intelligible throughout the world. They are, therefore, vulnerable to appropriation by only those segments of a non-western population who know and want western cooperative forms. Rotating associations are more familiar arrangements, yet are equitable enough to succeed.

2) Intermediate Organization. Relatively few existing informal associations lend themselves to direct formalization. Even the ones we have identified will not succeed as formalized groups unless members consider the new organization and its purposes fully acceptable. This likelihood is greatest where the new institutional commitments imposed on individuals are actually modeled on the informal associational patterns that they already know. The more extensively new formal roles and requirements are mediated through structurally acceptable middle-rung organizations, the greater their potential efficacy. If a women's rotating credit association is to become the basis, say, for an income-generating credit group, or a seed-loan scheme, it will only remain acceptable to participants if the personnel it introduces are familiar and perform accepted roles, if no new hierarchies are introduced, if the ostensible goals are shared by participants, if leadership continues to rotate and is not eroded by an overriding obligation to outside authority, and so on. Organization, though routinized, should still allow for flexibility.

These issues become particularly salient if we consider how to link new local-level groups to development institutions at higher levels of organization. The problem of providing such access to informally organized people without destroying their defenses and strengths is the central dilemma of this study. Development projects must be part of broader support schemes that provide participants with access to further educational or material assistance, or ensure that supply routes do not dry up, and the like. But linkages to other institutions can skew the primary relationships among members of informal associations and undermine local ingenuity.

In instances where development projects are based on the mobilization of informal associations as core groups for promoting local change, we can look to the principles underlying informal associations themselves as structural models. Informal associations, for instance, are animated by a mutual compact among members. If the men and women who staff middle-level development organizations do not merely represent the state or other external agencies, but depend significantly on the evaluation of their local constituency for their position (or for, say, salary increases or promotion), such two-way commitments between staff directors and local communities might build popular trust and involvement.

Other features of informal associations that might merit replication at higher levels of organization are flexibility of purpose and shifting leadership. Flexible purposes would allow regional and local offices to deal with community crises as they arose and grant them enough authority to marshall a variety of resources when necessary. Rotating leadership, an alternative to single power brokers, is another lesson to be garnered from informal associations and the ways in which they retain the mutual interdependence of members. Indeed, most of the qualities of informal associations discussed in the first five chapters can serve as inspirational models for formal development.

Any attempt to transform women's informal associations into intermediate organizations for change must be carefully qualified. Only a relatively small number of associational bases are appropriate models, and building on them requires a unique organizational approach. No uniform policy advocating the formalization of women's organizations as a means for the representation, politicization, and integration of women is appropriate.

Indeed, the western 'club' or voluntary association is often not the best vehicle for promoting development among disadvantaged populations. Where such associations have been established, they have imposed largely unfamiliar organizational roles. In scale, structure, and style most of them have been too large, too rationally bureaucratic, and too formal to be meaningful to members experienced only in the ways of informal associations. In Europe and the United States, to be sure, women have gained valuable political and economic experience through formal voluntary associations. Ironically, however, the very reasons that have made voluntary associations an effective crucible for feminism, political activism, and wide-ranging participation in public life for western women may also render them inappropriate to many nonwestern settings.

Women's voluntary associations emerged in the west as a direct result of industrialization and the privatization of women's worlds. Many women responded to their shared isolation by reaffirming their mutual bonds in voluntary and philanthropic organizations. Although women's voluntary associations have often rallied women into political participation and cooperation, they have emerged out of and alongside the privatized domestic sphere, and have in many ways continued to affirm those limits on women's place. In settings where the women's world is not privatized, the establishment of associations that are predicated on the trivialization of women's sphere will either remain unintelligible and alien, or may foretell an even greater cost, by proliferating western models for the domestication of women.

To the extent that voluntary associations do not completely rationalize all relations among member women, they have also reproduced and
reinforced many asymmetrical, hierarchical, and nonegalitarian informal
relationships (Marsot 1978). Philanthropic associations have typically
been a response of upper- and middle-class women, and have tended to
display and protect rank. They have largely perpetuated rather than
ended the marginality of client women on charity rolls. Established
largely under missionary and colonial influence, many of them have only
advanced the interests of women in a particular class. Caplan's account
of women's organizations in Madras, India, is representative of a widespread phenomenon. It shows how such associations "manufacture the
cultural elaboration of class positions in their major function of adminis-
tering charity to the poor" (1979: 28). Cohen (1979), comparing Creole
women in Sierra Leone who organize Old Girls' Dances with English
women on a housing estate, similarly finds that women's solidarity in both
cases is a ruse for the protection of class privilege.

APPROPRIATE ORGANIZATION FOR INTERVENTION

Limits to Mobilization

There are, then, well-defined structural limits on how far or how
closely we can build on existing linkages between formal and informal
associations. The interstitial women who indirectly channel goods,
services, or information from formal institutions to informal ones represent fragile connections: they balance their representative functions
finely between internal and external legitimacy. Any expansion or
regulation of their mediating role is restricted by the structural position
of such leadership. Difficulties also arise when, in activating or improv-
ing institutional linkages, we translate 'integration' into 'formalization.'
Formalization appears logical enough as long as we mean to replicate the
western shift to modernity through the elaboration, in E. Wolf's phrase,
of "non-agricultural corporate units :..which, though originally com-
mercial or artisan-kinship organizations, developed the organizational
potential of the corporate business structure" (Wolf 1966: 4). The appeal
of formalization as a policy is apparent, for it acknowledges the informal
sphere without relinquishing the primary commitment to institution-
building.
As a wide-ranging strategy for development, though, planned
formalization of organizations and roles is limited because it overlooks
the internal structural integrity of informal associations. It not only fails
to distinguish among informal associations, but it simultaneously belittles
the basic distinctions between formal and informal relationships. To be
sure, the boundary between the two is highly permeable, and some
informal associations — including those that are classically called 'voluntary associations' -- approximate formal ones, and can lend themselves to
effective formalization. Despite this permeability, however, and despite
the fact that informal associations perform many of the same political
and economic functions as formal institutions, often with comparable
legitimacy, both the routinization of personal linkages and the formalization of groups by definition efface the characteristics that distinguish
informal from formal. Implicit in such policies, then, is a disregard for or

a disparagement of the very features that we have portrayed as the sources of informal strength.

Since women in informal associations are pledged to one another through a multiplicity of cross-cutting, highly personal relations, integrative efforts that undermine the legitimacy of their associations can therefore be counterproductive. If the locus of legitimacy in any given development project rests within a formal bureaucracy, if personal obligations are replaced by strictly contractual ones as a basis for leadership organization, women stand to lose more than they can gain. Existing informal associations make poor 'targets', or 'engines' to harness, because it is the responsiveness and energy of the human relationships within them which drive them, and not their abstract existence or organization.

Strategies for the formalization of linkages between formal and informal associations, then, turn the problem on its head. They raise difficulties not only by ignoring the distinctions we have stressed between active and defensive associations on one hand and between egalitarian and asymmetrical ones on the other. More fundamentally, they evoke images of informal associations that are more bounded and also more fully divorced from the formal sphere than they generally are. While, as analysts and planners, we once perceived informal associations as everything that formal organizations were not, and thus neglected them, we now run the opposite risk of attributing too many of the characteristics of formal structures to the informal sphere. Such an interpretation of informal associations makes it easier, of course, to integrate them into our plans using the techniques and organizational style we already know. But, in most cases, it undermines the essential sources of strength within informal associations.

New Avenues for Change

Direct mobilization of informal leaders and associations is limited to a small subset of the informal sphere. Instead of reinforcing existing linkages between formal and informal organizations, another alternative is to create separate, new formal associations that parallel and grow out of existing informal commitments. The principle here is not unlike our recommendations for intermediate organizations, but the applications are more extensive. Existing informal associations should be well researched, not so they can be harnessed through either personal or institutional links to any development plan, but to inform the design of new appropriate associations. Appropriate informal associations then become models for new organizations: they are appropriate both because they are patterned after locally familiar forms and because they structure new equitable active relations without jeopardizing prior local resilience.

Depending on the cultural and historical context, recommendations such as the establishment of women's organizations, the expansion of formal and non-formal education and training, and the encouragement of small-group self-help projects do not necessarily have to mobilize the existing informal associations or recruit explicitly from them. They can create new collectivities patterned after familiar ones. Such programs can have a positive impact if they are organizationally sensitive and appropriate to their environment.

To devise schemes that suit both the internal needs and organizational limits demonstrated by informal associational patterns, we must take account of the following considerations:

Initially, we need to explore the purposes of the informal associations in any given community, to discover the felt needs of participants and identify attainable goals. This is not to recommend a strictly 'felt-needs' approach whereby women's expressed desires automatically become project goals. It does suggest, however, that because women's informal groupings typically coalesce purposively (that is, they do things together) and are not simply expressive or random, an understanding of the kinds of functions around which women commonly organize can help inform us of their needs and the ways in which they seek to satisfy these needs. Analysis of these functions can be useful in determining the issue or issues around which projects are to be organized.

Do women, for example, need to rely on each other most for child care? Can existing child-care patterns suggest models for additional care arrangements to free women for other activities? Do borrowing and lending networks allow women to perform necessary family jobs such as spinning wool or brewing beer? Or do they allow women to undertake income-producing activities, like weaving for sale, or pressing oil for the market? If more, or more efficient, appropriate technology (a new spinning wheel, still, loom, or oil press) were introduced, would these networks constitute an appropriate organization to carry it through to effective use?

The investigation of such questions can shed much light on appropriate issues and organization of development programs. In places where women only rarely share in labor rotation or labor sharing — as among the Yanomamo Indians, for example (Shapiro 1976) — programs modelled on labor exchange would be futile. Where women have wide-ranging, society-wide communication networks -- as in the case of the Shahsevan nomads (Tapper 1978) — use of mass communication techniques may be mandated; where networks tend to be narrower, or where information is at a premium and circulates less freely, such techniques would not be appropriate.

Next, an understanding of the bases of informal associations can also suggest effective organizational principles. Often, informal associational patterns differ greatly from the group identities we might expect to find if we looked only for loyalties based on formal institutional categories. By paying attention to the shape of informal solidarities and personal affiliations that women activate to attain various goals, we can help ensure that projects take advantage of those local sodalities that are in line with redistributive and developmental goals, instead of unwittingly hurting group strengths.

Thus, where vertical intergenerational ties among women predominate -- as in the Muslim Middle East -- different policies on family planning (or education and training) may be more appropriate than in places where peer relationships are strong -- as in the age-grade traditions of Africa. Where women's networks consistently cross sectarian barriers — as they have in working-class districts of Beirut or in Galilean Arab villages — we do not need to deliver health care or other social services through sectarian organizations, despite their greater visibility (Joseph 1975; Rosenfeld 1974). Where single-sex associations are more commonplace than mixed-sex associations, this too can guide planners.

While these suggestions all seem fairly obvious, they bear repetition. The emphasis on formal organizations and politics has produced a skewed impression that women have few associational ties available outside the domestic arena. Even when the rich relationships within women's worlds are acknowledged, they are more often understood as normative systems to be overcome, or as guarantors of social control, rather than purposive and rational arrangements which might provide organizational models for appropriate social planning. Shantytown neighborhood solidarity among kinswomen and neighbors, for example, can be mobilized around such issues as child care, living conditions, better education, and consumer issues (Safa 1976).

Field researchers must also begin to imagine what types of new organizations would suit the specific case in question. One critical measure of this appropriateness is the fit between the organizational style of the proposed development programs and that of the pre-existing informal associations among the people they aim to reach. It is clear that the wholesale imposition of western models for the organization of family, community, and work will not produce appropriate or creative development planning for women. It is equally apparent that many existing informal associations among women do not promote development goals of equal opportunity, increased access to resources and self-rule. We propose a third approach: that development planners identify, among existing informal associations, those which embody both the internal and external relations conducive to increased opportunity and equity, then attempt to replicate such relations in new project-sponsored associations.

Finally, if appropriate projects that reach women are to be successful, women's associational ties must remain accessible and not subject to distortion or blockage -- whether by men, by powerful women, or by a concentration of other self-interested clusters. The way that such projects are organized into the broader setting, and the linkages that connect them to higher levels of institutional authority, must in turn adhere to the principles of intermediate organization outlined earlier in this chapter.

Approach by Analogy

Women's existing informal associations do not typically provide either leaders or groups that are ready-made for mobilization in external development efforts. Except in the restricted instances discussed above, the vitality of most women's associations cannot be tapped by simply hitching them into development harnesses; most of the time, such parasitism destroys the very organizational and leadership strengths that make women's informal associations attractive to development planning and implementation in the first place.

This does not mean that women's informal associations have no place in planned development, but it does mean that their involvement must be carefully evaluated. One of the most effective approaches for accomplishing this utilizes knowledge about the informal organization of women's worlds to establish new associations, modelled explicitly upon those existing ones that correspond most closely with development objectives. This avenue for incorporating women's informal associations into development might be called organization by analogy: it creates new associations parallel to old ones; these new associations replicate the desirable structural features of old ones, but are still separate from them; and, finally, the new associations are more purposefully dedicated toward development change.

The design of programs to complement, but not commandeer, appropriate informal associational patterns represents an approach by analogy, using knowledge about informal associations to reach a better understanding of where women's needs lie and what form of social organization may best answer those needs. By creating parallel associations that are homologous to, but not isomorphic with existing ones, this approach takes advantage of the informal strengths -- flexibility, purposiveness and responsiveness to member needs -- without encroaching directly upon the fragility of existing informal alliances. Such an approach would build upon familiar social forms, but replicate only those aspects -- of their active, focused and equitable economic purposiveness -- which are consonant with development objectives. Drawing upon the examples of "appropriate" or "intermediate" technologies (Schumacher 1973), organizationally "appropriate" associations would be designed so that their indigenous familiarity allowed them to remain socially and culturally intelligible to participants, on the one hand, while, on the other, introducing some organizational shifts toward more equitable and autonomous associational forms.

Close inspection of case studies of successful women's projects reveals that they often, consciously or unconsciously, adopted a similar strategy for development. The Korean Mothers' Clubs discussed earlier (Chapter 6) thus did not take over pre-existing informal associations, but they did organize women who had previous ties with one another and previous experience in traditional savings associations.

> The mothers' club concept is not new to Korean society. Prior to the Korean government's declaration of a population policy in 1961, traditional informal associations existed in Korean villages to provide women with social contacts and cooperative savings pools. These associations, known as Kae, were comprised of friends who met every month to pool their financial resources. One member at each meeting would be given access to the savings pool. The Kae thereby provided village women with useful experience in organization, group participation and cohesiveness, and contributed directly to the formal introduction of village-level group such as the mothers' club (Lee 1976: 5).

The Wok Meri investment and exchange groups, initiated by women in the Eastern Highlands of Papua, New Guinea, have similarly drawn on women's previous associational ties with one another (Sexton 1980a and b; Singh 1974). These groups, which originated in the 1960s, have taken over the rituals of birth and marriage, the payment of bridewealth, and other aspects of traditional pig feasts. Although the Wok Meri groups represent a dramatically new and successful social form, devoted to saving and investing money, they have proliferated largely because of the transfigured rituals they have adopted. Many of these turn on women's reproductive role and identity, which came to encompass new and expanded meanings in the transformative process. The Wok Meri, according to

Sexton, is a conscious "demonstration of women's competence that is also meant to encourage men to follow women's example" (1980b: 5).

As a general strategy, then, the replication of appropriate associations by analogy of existing ones has far wider application than direct intervention or the mobilization of informal associations as ready-made vehicles for development. As groups to mobilize directly, women's informal associations are largely inappropriate vehicles for development, but as organizational models for development by analogy, those associations which meet the criteria of activeness, purposiveness and equity can provide vital patterns for replicable appropriate organization.

Evaluating Strategies for Intervention: Which is Right?

There are several essential questions to ask before involving any particular informal association in a wider strategy for intervention. These questions provide a framework for evaluating (1) whether the association being considered is appropriate for development at all and (2) where intervention appears feasible, whether it would proceed best (a) through direct mobilization of existing groups or group leaders, or (b) through the design of new associations by analogy to the strongest features of old ones. No single strategy for development intervention is right in all cases; indeed, several different approaches are likely to be required.

The diagram on the following page (Figure 2, p. 116) is intended to highlight the issues that must be addressed when reaching women through any informal avenue is contemplated. The evaluation of the different strategies outlined in this monograph for development for women begins, of course, only after the various features of existing women's informal associations have been identified (as summarized in Figure 1, p. 46). Once the underlying indigenous structures have been identified, a second sequence of questions may assist in deciding which avenues for development are appropriate.

The first overarching question investigates the nature of the linkages between women's existing informal associations and the formal governmental or development bureaucracies concerned with intervention. As we have seen, those linkages may be both personal — operating through individuals who act as political, economic and cultural brokers or intermediaries — or the links may be institutional — operating directly with groups because of their activities as groups.

Some personal linkages act primarily to protect a vulnerable constituency, as in the cases of many of the midwives, curers and the 'arifa discussed earlier. In such cases, women's informal associations are characteristically "defensive" self-help associations. Their leadership cannot be drafted into development efforts without serious damage to the underlying defensive compact between leader and constituency. When such leaders are additionally asked to broker for a development or government bureaucracy, they are either ineffective or lose local legitimacy, depending, respectively, upon whether they retain their fundamental allegiance to their original clients or shift it to become lowest-level functionaries in the formal bureaucracy.

Other personal linkages can act both to protect and to communicate client needs. Such leaders are often effective in obtaining goods and services from the formal bureaucracies for their constituency. The associations they lead display those features characteristic of "active" women's associations. Their leaders, like the opinion leaders, mayors and political party leaders already discussed, are linked to the formal spheres two-directionally, communicating local needs to formal authorities and delivering needed goods and services back to their local community. As effective as these active leaders at times are, giving them a role in planned development is not always desirable.

Such personal intermediaries are, of course, often not even-handed in the distribution of the fruits of their positions; often, as has been seen, personal links lead primarily to personal profit and the further entrenchment of local elites. But, as well, when formal government or development authorities lack local-level legitimacy, empowering local leaders, who in such cases are accountable to neither their local community nor to the formal bureaucracies, may simply result in ever more effective systems of local graft and extortion. When, however, personal linkages exist in a climate of local opinion that generally acknowledges the legitimacy of wider development and government agencies, even though it may not be appropriate to channel new resources directly through local informal leaders, it is often entirely appropriate, and extremely effective, to channel information through them. Although checks must be made to assure a continuing two-way flow of information, the traditional role of local informal leadership in shaping community consensus lends itself well to conveying new development information as well.

In general, though, the constraints on personal leaders in even relatively "active" informal associations limit their effectiveness as linkages into or for formal development efforts. Greater opportunities for building upon the strengths of women's informal associations emerge when those associations have, or can develop, links with formal governmental and development agencies through their activities as collectivities rather than through the personal ties of individuals.

All informal associations are not, of course, alike in their potential for development: some, especially the more defensive, cannot be effectively reached or incorporated by development; others, if developed, would lead to undesirable changes in the local communities, especially where resources are not equitably distributed within existing informal associastions. In order to evaluate the potential for incorporating a specific group into development efforts, each must first be assessed with respect to the criteria for identifying women's informal associations that were outlined earlier (see Figure 1, p. 46). As we have seen, many existing informal associations are too defensive, too diffuse, or focused too exclusively on ritual or religious activities to be appropriate for development. Even among those more active associations focused upon more explicitly economic activities, only those which are structured so as to redistribute resources equitably — like rotating credit or labor associations — present indigenous organizations with real potential for development.

In some cases, this development can be direct or nearly so, resulting in the formalization of existing groups within government or development bureaucracies. In most cases, however, if only because so few local groups actually fulfill all our criteria for structure and equity, it is more likely that development should proceed by creating new groups, by "analogy" as described above. These new groups would be clearly modelled on those among the existing ones that most closely approximate our criteria, but slightly modified to make the approximation even closer.

No single avenue for the development of women's informal associations is always right. Neither, however, is the choice among the various avenues a matter of pure or arbitrary discretion. Instead, we have argued, first, that it is possible to describe women's existing informal associations in such a way as to highlight their potential for development explicitly, and, second, that it is possible on the basis of that description to evaluate whether or how to incorporate each into development change.

A first glance at our conclusions (especially as summarized n the two tree diagrams, Figures 1 & 2) may appear discouraging, restricting as we do the avenues for development. Clearly, however, the point of development is not change for the sake of any change, but directed change. We hold firm on two principles. First, we are committed to supporting a style of change that builds upon the familiar in order both to lessen the social and cultural dislocation of change to local peoples and, as well, to enhance the chances that our changes will be successfully adopted by them. Second, we have structured our criteria and questions for evaluating women's informal associations in such a way that only those changes which will reach and circulate new resources equitably among the most vulnerable people without jeopardizing their position further are supported

Informal associations do not provide a pre-organized group ready-made to mobilize or harness, but can serve rather as an important baseline of data to help anchor developmental activities in familiar social reality. Analysis of the informal sphere can help shape projects that conform not simply to the obvious dictates of governments, change agencies, or well organized social groups, but also to the less visible and less audible informal associations that structure the lives of the poor.

The design of programs that are complementary and appropriate to informal associational patterns represents an approach by analogy, using knowledge about informal associations to reach a better understanding of where women's needs lie and what form of social organization may best answer those needs. It thus takes advantage of the informal strengths -- flexibility, purposiveness and responsiveness to member needs -- without encroaching on the fragility and vulnerability of interpersonal ties. As a general strategy, the replication of appropriate associations within development projects probably has far wider application than direct intervention or the mobilization of informal associations as ready-made groups. As groups to mobilize they are largely inappropriate, but as organizational models, informal associations which meet our criteria of activeness, purposiveness and equity may suggest patterns for replicable appropriate organization.

The essential questions which need to be answered before involving any particular informal association in a wider strategy for intervention are summarized in the following tree diagram (Figure 2 on next page). Once the internal structure of an informal association has been evaluated (see Figure 1, p. 52), these additional questions must be asked about the potential implications of the different ways in which informal associations can be embedded within, or interface with, formal government or development bureaucracies. As this figure demonstrates, there are two primary avenues for the integration of women's informal associations into development: one (the more limited) revolves around the transformation of existing associations into intermediate groups; the other (more promising) requires the creation of new appropriate groups modeled upon familiar informal associations:

116

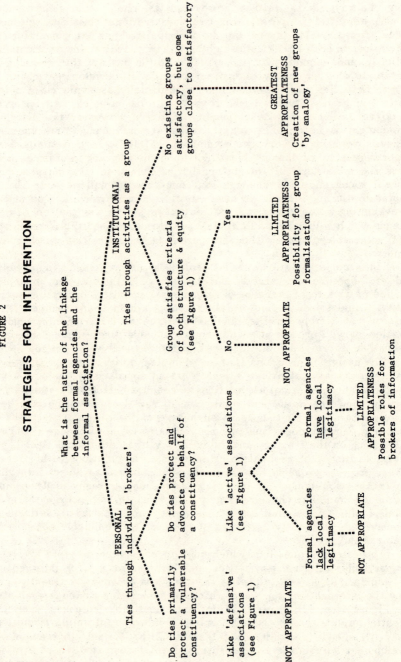

FIGURE 2

STRATEGIES FOR INTERVENTION

What is the nature of the linkage
between formal agencies and the
informal association?

PERSONAL
Ties through individual 'brokers'

INSTITUTIONAL
Ties through activities as a group

Do ties primarily
protect a vulnerable
constituency?

Do ties protect and
advocate on behalf of
a constituency?

Group satisfies criteria
of both structure & equity
(see Figure 1)

No existing groups
satisfactory, but some
groups close to satisfactory

Like 'defensive'
associations
(see Figure 1)

Like 'active' associations
(see Figure 1)

No

Yes

NOT APPROPRIATE

Formal agencies
lack local
legitimacy

Formal agencies
have local
legitimacy

NOT APPROPRIATE

LIMITED
APPROPRIATENESS
Possible roles for
brokers of information

NOT APPROPRIATE

LIMITED
APPROPRIATENESS
Possibility for group
formalization

GREATEST
APPROPRIATENESS
Creation of new groups
'by analogy'

COMPLEXITY IN CHANGE

The design of new appropriate organizations plainly requires a holistic appraisal of informal associations -- one that takes account of change and recognizes the delicate balances within informal associations. Not all of the purposes that are served by informal associations can or need to be met through alternative, formalized organizations. It is a matter of judgment to determine which associational strengths to complement.

It is to help guide such judgments that this monograph has been written. We have urged that the varied bases of solidarity and legitimacy underlying women's associations be scrutinized. How do they correspond with overarching ranking systems within a society on one hand, and prevailing patterns of gender relationships on the other? The more nearly informal associations reproduce these hierarchies and accept their legitimacy, the less likely they are to provide effective alternatives to an unfavorable status quo.

At the same time, it is impossible to overlook the flexibility and innovative potential even of conservative associations. Neither the basis for collective action nor the institutional settings that condition that action should be regarded as static. Especially in situations of rapid change, defensive associations may enable women to challenge or transmute some of the seemingly restrictive customs that lie at the core of many women's religious and cultural traditions. Fallers and Fallers (1976) have made precisely this point about women's solidary groups in Turkey. They argue that women's support groups, rooted in the traditional women's world and the segregation of the sexes, have actually smoothed the entry of Turkish women into the labor force (following Ataturk's legal reforms). M. Wolf (1974) has similarly suggested that the political activism of Chinese women during and after their revolution was actually honed for centuries by their experience in manipulating uterine family ties and their long-time skills in shaping village opinion. The Wok Meri exchange system provides another vivid illustration of an informal association that has responded to changed economic circumstances by redefining customary rituals to serve pioneering ends (Sexton 1980 a and b).

In Mombasa, Kenya, traditional lelemama dance societies, popular among Muslim women until the 1950s, also enabled women to respond dynamically to change. As Strobel (1976) has shown, women participated in dance groups partly for status considerations. In a society that was preoccupied with socially ascribed hierarchy, the lelemama associations provided them with an "alternative set of status distinctions and rewards apart from descent. (Dance groups) offered prestige to women who had few other sources of dignity and honor" (Strobel 1976: 192). Ultimately, however, dance group prestige did little to alter women's actual social standing and possibly even helped to entrench the existing hierarchy by offering slaves and poor women a purely symbolic outlet for political, social or economic frustration. Because the groups were inherently competitive, moreover, the dissidence they fostered often exacerbated ethnic cleavages among participants and observers of dance contests. Like parallel groups elsewhere, the Mombasa dance associations served as instruments of social control, reinforcing norms by singing about misdeeds and their punishment.

Despite these traditional foundations for dance-group cohesion, Strobel has suggested that the lelemama associations actually stimulated women to adopt new attitudes and promoted a certain amount of change through various means. They encouraged the acquisition of new skills by providing a focal point for the mobilization of people, finances, and equipment at times of celebration. They allowed for considerable expression of rebellion: elite women danced alongside poor women, and all women could dance in nontraditional dress, without their customary black robes. In an important sense, Strobel argues, lelemama associations constituted the precursors for the women's political and cultural organizations that began to develop in the 1950s.[1]

Still, the paradoxical capacity of women's associations to reinforce male dominance is not easy to resolve. The charge of supporting sexual inequality has been most frequently laid against defensive associations, particularly when they coalesce around events, like childbirth, which encapsulate elements of the prevailing ideology of male dominance. Many writers have similarly interpreted women's ritual and religious activities as props for sexual asymmetry in preindustrial settings. As we have discussed, not all analysts concur in this assessment. MacCormack (Hoffer), for example, chooses to emphasize the vital collective heritage that Mende and Sherbo women impart to one another through the Sande society, even though this tradition is partly based on ritual clitoridectomy (1975, 1980). The ideological sources of women's strengths simultaneously constitute the structural limits on sexual parity. This is an irony that grows out of the interdependence of dominant men and subordinate women. But the traditions that give women cultural value "while also setting women apart as oppressed" (Rapp 1979: 512) cannot easily be reformed from outside without destroying the whole fabric of solidarity and strength in which they are embedded.

Social structures as well as ideologies have a dialectic of their own. Joseph (1976), for example, has shown that women's egalitarian and non-sectarian street networks in a working-class suburb of Beirut have ultimately served to reinforce sectarian politics in Lebanon. Women's networks have replicated the very mixed residence patterns of the quarter, whose inhabitants ordinarily tolerate intermarriage even between Christians and Muslims. Joseph, however, concludes that these women's networks cannot be interpreted as counter-institutions created by women in response to their exclusion from political and legal processes. Women are not that strong. On the contrary, they must revert to the only avenues of influence that are open to them whenever they need special favors or judgments, turning to leading families within their own particular sects. They support the very patronage ties that maintain a sectarian political system.

This case provides a good illustration of the need to supplement our analytical categories with a nuanced consideration of the different forces that operate on informal networks and the various processes that such networks generate in turn. The Beirut street networks, while at first glance active and egalitarian, also have important roles in protecting the vulnerability of neighborhood residents. It is in this capacity that they activate asymmetrical ties with sectarian notables and expand the support base of the sectarian political leadership.

---

[1]These later organizations, it must be added, never developed into feminist associations.

By themselves, the labels "defensive" or "asymmetrical" do not fully represent the dynamics of these associations. Examining the sometimes intricate linkages between formal and informal structures is the only way to determine which of these features is most salient in what context. The place of informal ties within the overall system also suggests both the kinds of programs that might be appropriate as well as some that might not. Local-level health services, for example, might effectively be offered through a non-sectarian organization, while the street networks themselves would probably form a poor basis for a working-class associ-ation.

Processes of change have deeply affected women's associational styles and must also be taken into account. In particular, changes resulting from the introduction of capital or its asymmetrical accumula-tion, the formation of sharpened class interests, and the consolidation of state structures have had great impact not only on the sexual division of labor, but also on women's informal associations based partly on that division of labor. Rosenfeld (1974) has demonstrated this in his analysis of visiting patterns among Arab village women in Israel. Village men worked away from home for wages, and their relationships among themselves were largely hierarchical, reflecting differences in wealth and power. Women, however, took care to keep their visits and relationships with one another reciprocal. They tended to be extremely egalitarian and eclectic in their associational patterns, often crossing sectarian barriers and refusing to acknowledge keen status distinctions. As inequalities among the villagers were heightened over a period of twenty years, though, Rosenfeld suggests that prevailing associational patterns also shifted. When women visit today, they do so increasingly as representatives of their husbands' class position. In fact, visits or gifts have come to be exchanged among conjugal pairs more often than among the women on their own. In this instance, any social plan that aims either to draw upon or to support the eclectic egalitarianism of women's associations has to counter the emerging wider tendencies toward social hierarchy (see also Benedict 1974 and Kandiyoti 1977).

Our discussion has compressed long and uneven processes of social change into a somewhat flattened mould. But the criteria it has evolved for assessing the potential for informal associations in change do not require us to conceptualize strictly dichotomous types of association. Active and defensive, equitable and asymmetrical, institutional and counter-institutional -- these aspects of informal associations represent countervailing tendencies rather than mutually exclusive categories. They can provide us with a general sense of what informal associations are or do; but they lose their utility if we reduce them to a mechanistic index. Each case must be considered on its own, not only in terms of its internal dynamism and autonomous dimension, but also in light of the varied linkages that connect it to the formal institutional sphere.

8

Some Concluding Guidelines

> Americans of all ages, all conditions and all dispositions constantly form associations. They have not only commercial and manufacturing companies in which all take part, but associations of a thousand other kinds. If it is proposed to inculcate some truth or foster some feeling by encouragement of the great example, they form a society. Nothing in my opinion is more deserving of our attention than the intellectual and moral associations of America.
>
> --Alexis de Tocqueville, Democracy in America

Informal associations simultaneously promote women's political influence and economic contributions on the one hand and their subordination, victimization or exclusion on the other. The internal dynamics of women's informal associations explain neither the origins of nor the variations in women's position; these can be better accounted for in light of the linkages between formal and informal spheres. But an appreciation of informal organizational patterns makes women visible and marks their influence in a way that theories focusing narrowly on formal organizations cannot.

By identifying women's activities within the informal sphere, we are not just locating the place where they occur. We are defining those activities as partly autonomous, possessing power in their own right, and deriving vitality and legitimacy from a mutual compact among members. This reoriented perception of the informal sphere runs counter to the rhetoric of bureaucratic rationalization pervading public policy in the west.

Studying women's informal associations in rural development has therefore required a reconciliation of contradictory themes. 'Development,' especially for marginal populations, entails more formal organization -- of production and delivery systems, of more regular access between centers of power and their peripheries, and of the constituencies of the poor themselves. But despite our own historical confidence in the power of rationalized organization, informal associations typically resist incorporation into formal organizations. If formalized, many of the most diffuse associations will evaporate; others risk losing their unique strengths of flexibility and mutuality. Depending on the nature of the external authority that subsumes them, they stand to lose their internal cohesion and legitimacy as well.

To help resolve these contradictions, this monograph has proposed that informal associations be plotted along a conceptual continuum between associations that use defensive tactics at one extreme, and those which are capable of more active, self-assertive and autonomous strategies at the other. Associations that are primarily limited to strategies of defensive self-protection cannot be successfully reached by or incorporated into externally organized enterprises; intervention makes such associations more vulnerable and tends to force them further underground.

But if defensive associations are a uniformly inappropriate locus for intervention, this does not necessarily mean that active informal associations are therefore a uniformly good place to begin. There are two additional features of women's active informal associations that determine their suitability for intervention. First, those informal women's associations which have more narrowly organized their activities around economic or political purposes must be identified. This explicitness of purpose is important for two reasons. It concentrates the impact of development within its intended domains of economic resources and political organizational skills. There is also less danger of reinforcing unknown social, political, or economic relations if the association itself is less diffuse.

Second, among those informal associations which focus upon restricted economic and political purposes, we must determine which are structured so as to redistribute any introduced resources equitably. To determine which among the active women's informal associations will respond best to new resources, there are a number of specific questions we can ask. Although we are basically concerned that the organizational structure of the association reflect and protect the interests of all members equally, there are at least two separable issues at play here. First, we must ascertain whether the association, as it exists, works to distribute its resources fairly among all its members, or whether, instead of equal redistribution, it in fact produces increasing disparities among members. And, second, we need to know whether the internal structure of association politics ensures that all members participate equally in or have equal access to group decision-making procedures and avenues of redress.

Once this identification is made, one way of reaching informal associations is to strengthen ties with leaders or key personalities within them. It bears repeating that recruitment of such informal leaders is only feasible in the case of equitable associations that engage in active strategies. Wealthy patrons will not make the best representatives for their clients' interests (theirs is an inequitable alliance); and midwives or curers can rarely maintain the trust of their clients if they assume additional contractual obligations to outside authority (for theirs was a primarily defensive association). Even in active and equitable associations, however, the interstitial position of leaders, who represent the membership on one hand and act as agents of external authority on the other, is finely balanced. In any dealings with such leaders, then, the importance of preserving local initiative and autonomy is paramount lest the local credibility of leaders be destroyed.

The circulation of information and skills through intermediate local leaders is more advisable than the introduction of new resources through them. Whether an association is diffuse or sharply bounded, and regardless of its central purposes or internal structure, it provides participants with communication networks. As we seek to involve women's informal associations in communication for development, however, we must also recognize the ways in which information becomes a source of power. In any setting where 'knowing someone' is a key requirement for getting something, the significance of contacts and connections intensifies. In the absence of formalized channels of communication and in situations where word of mouth is a primary medium, women's communication networks provide avenues to influence as well as information. They can hasten the spread of an idea or the adoption of an opinion.

If wide circulation of information is desired, pivotal women's influence cannot hinge on any newly established formal relationship with a development agency. Insofar as such women are perceived as part of a development bureaucracy, their local credibility diminishes. A client-centered approach is imperative in the design of communication projects that make use of informal ties among women. Information, moreover, must not be allowed to become a scarce commodity if equitable development is to proceed. While capitalizing on the potential influence of opinion leaders wherever possible, efforts at the diffusion of information should nevertheless not revolve too closely around them. In most cases, a more broadly based approach can be more productive.

A second way of building on informal associations is through small-group strategies. Some informal associations may themselves become effective bases for small groups that generate economic development. Small group strategies in many ways represent an intermediate level of organization. They respect and preserve the face-to-face nature of informal associations and are often well suited to capitalize on some informal associational strengths. Nevertheless, it is important to remember that only clearly bounded and highly structured informal associations lend themselves to this kind of formalization. Rotating labor and credit associations are probably the most likely of such groups to succeed.

Development interest in informal associations should not be limited to attempts to mobilize them directly. Informal associations can be most useful as a data base rather than an organizational base in the planning process. By understanding the nature and extent of informal associations among women in a given setting, analysts can gain important insights into the dynamics, structure, and possibilities of women's worlds. This does not necessarily involve detailed investigation of each woman's "support networks". In fact, a good case can be made against breaching the privacy of vulnerable defensive networks, except in cases where the investigator maintains a long-term presence in the community and is part of those networks. It is nevertheless important to acquire some understanding of the scope and character of women's informal associations, and to to recognize their broad significance.

Information about prevailing associational patterns among women can be used to design new 'appropriate associations.' Appropriate associational models would be based on those associations found in any given community that fulfilled the basic criteria for development suitability outlined in this monograph: capable of active strategies, purposively economic or political, and equitable in patterns for redistributing resources or power. Rather than tapping those associations themselves, either through leaders or as groups, development may best proceed by creating new analogous associations, 'appropriate' as vehicles for planned change because they both meet the planners' criteria for suitability and are familiar to participants. For example, one feature of informal associations that is promising, if difficult to replicate, is the mutual responsibility among their members. Fashioning mutual responsibilities between both local-level development organizations and the personnel of the next level of organization may be one of the best ways of ensuring devolution in development. Administrators, in other words, must be made to depend not just on their superiors but more importantly upon their local constituencies in some of the same ways that informal leaders owe service to their followers.

In designing new, appropriate organizations that are based on existing informal relationships, linkages between the formal and informal spheres must also be considered. The overall embeddedness of informal associations in social systems will influence attempts to integrate them. Social structures cannot be separated cleanly into formal institutions at the apex, where the powerful and privileged find affiliation, and informal associations at the bottom and margins, encompassing the poor. It would be more accurate to see both kinds of bonds as operating on all individuals at once -- although most women have fewer connections to modern, formal institutions than men do. Informal social ties thus exist throughout any society; and formal institutions generally extend linkages, however indirectly, to even the most marginal people. In building new linkages or reinforcing old ones, then, we must not only examine the particular linkages in question. It is also essential to probe the nature and full extent of the existing formal/informal nexus. Some overall linkage patterns, for example, promote social integration, but at the cost of equity, or of political and economic integration.

These are not simple guidelines. There are many historical examples of informal associations that have generated either great transformations, or resistance to change, but where the outcome was not predictable in advance. An awareness of the interdependence between formal and informal spheres cannot help us to engineer social change as we build a dam or dig an irrigation canal. It is not always possible to determine which -- the informal or the formal -- is logically prior to the other. The process whereby formal and informal associations interact and influence one another is a continuous two-way process. We can, however, reduce the unintended consequences of planned change if we learn to create new formal programs that complement, respect, and build on the many strengths that women have traditionally found within the informal sphere.

Bibliography

Abu-Lughod, J.
1961   Migrant adjustment to city life: the Egyptian case. AMERICAN JOURNAL OF SOCIOLOGY 67(1), pp. 22-32.

Anderson, Robert T.
1966   Rotating credit associations in India. ECONOMIC DEVELOPMENT AND CULTURAL CHANGE 14(3), pp. 334-339.

Ardener, Edwin
1977   Belief and the problem of women, and the 'problem' revisited. In S. Ardener, ed., PERCEIVING WOMEN. New York: John Wiley, (1972), pp. 1-27.

Ardener, Shirley
1964   The comparative study of rotating credit associations. JOURNAL OF THE ROYAL ANTHROPOLOGICAL IN- STITUTE 94, pp. 201-229.

1977   Sexual insult and female militancy. In. S. Ardener, ed., PERCEIVING WOMEN. New York: John Wiley, (1975, 1973), pp. 29-53.

✓ Arizpe, Lourdes
1977   Women in the informal labor sector: the case of Mexico City. SIGNS: JOURNAL OF WOMEN IN CULTURE AND SOCIETY 3(1), pp. 25-37.

Awe, Bolanle
1977   The Iyalode in the traditional Yoruba political system. In Alice Schlegel, ed., SEXUAL STRATIFICATION: A CROSS-CULTURAL VIEW. New York: Columbia Uni- versity Press, pp. 144-160.

Banck, Geert A.
1973   Network analysis and social theory. In J. Boissevain and J. Clyde Mitchell, eds., NETWORK ANALYSIS:

STUDIES IN HUMAN INTERACTION. The Hague: Mouton, pp. 37-44.

Barnes, James Allen.
1972   SOCIAL NETWORKS. Reading, Mass.: Addison-Wesley Publishing Co., Also Addison-Wesley module 26, pp. 1-29.

Bascom, William R.
1952   The Esusu: a credit institution of the Yoruba. JOURNAL OF THE ROYAL ANTHROPOLOGICAL INSTITUTE 82(1), pp. 63-69.

Benedict, P.
1974   The Kabul günü: structured visiting in an Anatolian provincial town. Anthropological Quarterly 47 (Jan.), pp. 28-47.

Berger, Iris
1976   Rebels or status-seekers? Women as spirit mediums in East Africa. In Hafkin and Bay, eds., WOMEN IN AFRICA: STUDIES IN SOCIAL AND ECONOMIC Change. Stanford, California: Stanford University Press, pp. 157-181.

Berger, Morrol
1961   The Arab danse du ventre. DANCE PERSPECTIVES 10, pp. 6-49.

Berreman, Gerald
1972   HINDUS OF THE HIMALAYAS: ETHNOGRAPHY AND CHANGE. Berkeley, Calif.: University of California Press.

Betteridge, Anne H.
1980   The controversial vows of urban Muslim women in Iran. In Nancy Falk and Rita Gross, eds., UNSPOKEN WORLDS: WOMEN'S RELIGIOUS LIVES IN NON-WESTERN CULTURES. San Francisco: Harper and Row Publishers, pp. 141-155.

Boissevain, Jeremy
1968   The place of non-groups in the social sciences. MAN 3, pp. 542-556.

Bolton, Ralph and Enrique Mayer
1977   ANDEAN KINSHIP AND MARRIAGE. Washington, D.C.: American Anthropological Association.

Boserup, Ester
1970   WOMEN'S ROLE IN ECONOMIC DEVELOPMENT. London: George Allen.

Bott, Elizabeth
1957   FAMILY AND SOCIAL NETWORKS: ROLES, NORMS, AND EXTERNAL RELATIONSHIPS IN ORDINARY URBAN FAMILIES. London: Tavistock Publishers.

Brana-Shute, Rosemary
1976   Women, clubs, and politics: the case of a lower-class neighborhood in Paramaribo, Suriname. URBAN ANTHROPOLOGY 5(2), pp. 157-186.

Briggs, Jean L.
1978   NEVER IN ANGER: PORTRAIT OF AN ESKIMO FAMILY. Cambridge, Mass.: Harvard University Press.

Brown, Judith K.
1969   Cross-cultural ratings of subsistence activities and sex division of labor: retrospects and prospects. BEHAVIORAL SCIENCE NOTES 4, pp. 281-290.

1975   Iroquois women: an ethnohistoric note. In Rayna R. Reiter, ed., TOWARD AN ANTHROPOLOGY OF WOMEN. New York: Monthly Review Press, pp. 235-251.

Bujra, Janet M.
1979   Introductory: female solidarity and the sexual division of labour. In Patricia Caplan and Janet M. Bujra, eds., WOMEN UNITED, WOMEN DIVIDED: COMPARATIVE STUDIES OF TEN CONTEMPORARY CULTURES. Bloomington: Indiana University Press, pp. 13-45.

Burkett, Elinor C.
1977   In dubious sisterhood: class and sex in Spanish Colonial South America. LATIN AMERICAN PERSPECTIVES 12 and 13, IV (1 and 2), pp. 18-26.

Campbell, Colin D. and Chang Shick Ahn
1962   Kyes and Mujins -- financial intermediaries in South Korea. ECONOMIC DEVELOPMENT AND CULTURAL CHANGE 10 (3), pp. 55-68.

Caplan, Patricia
1979   Women's organizations in Madras City, India. In Patricia Caplan and Janet M. Bujra, eds., WOMEN UNITED, WOMEN DIVIDED: COMPARATIVE STUDIES OF TEN CONTEMPORARY CULTURES. Bloomington: Indiana University Press, pp. 99-128.

Chaney, Elsa M.
1973   Women in Latin American politics: the case of Peru and Chile. In Pescatello, ed., FEMALE AND MALE IN LATIN AMERICA. Pittsburgh: University of Pittsburgh Press, pp. 103-139.

Cohen, Gaynor
1979 Women's solidarity and the preservation of privilege. In Patricia Caplan and Janet M. Bujra, eds., WOMEN UNITED, WOMEN DIVIDED: COMPARATIVE STUDIES OF TEN CONTEMPORARY CULTURES. Bloomington: Indiana University Press, pp. 129-156.

Cornelisen, Ann.
1977 WOMEN OF THE SHADOWS. Boston: Little, Brown and Company.

Cronin, Constance
1977 Illusion and reality in Sicily. In Alice Schlegel, ed., SEXUAL STRATIFICATION: A CROSS-CULTURAL VIEW. New York: Columbia University Press, pp. 67-93.

Daly, Mary
1978 GYN/ECOLOGY. Boston: Beacon Books.

Douglas, Mary
1971 Is matriliny doomed in Africa? In Mary Douglas and Phyllis M. Kaberry, eds., MAN IN AFRICA. London: Tavistock, pp. 123-137.

Draper, P.
1975 !Kung women: contrasts in sexual egalitarianism in foraging and sedentary contexts. In Rayna R. Reiter, ed., TOWARD AN ANTHROPOLOGY OF WOMEN. New York: Monthly Review Press, pp. 77-109.

Dubisch, Jill
1977 The mother-daughter tie in mediterranean social structure. Paper presented at the AAA meeting, Houston.

Dwyer, Daisy Hilse
1977 Bridging the gap between the sexes in Moroccan legal practice. In Alice Schlegel, ed., SEXUAL STRATIFICATION: A CROSS-CULTURAL VIEW. New York: Columbia University Press, pp. 41-66.

1978 Women, Sufism, and decision-making in Moroccan Islam. In Lois Beck and Nikki Keddie, eds., WOMEN IN THE MUSLIM WORLD. Cambridge, Mass.: Harvard University Press, pp. 585-598.

Dyson-Hudson, Rada
1960 Men, women and work in a pastoral society. NATURAL HISTORY 69 (10), pp. 42-56.

Embree, John
1946 SUYE MURA. London: Kegan Paul.

Etienne, Mona and Eleanor Leacock
    1980   WOMEN AND COLONIZATION: ANTHROPOLOGICAL PERSPECTIVES. New York: Praeger Publishers.

Fakhouri, H.
    1968   The Zar cult in an Egyptian village. ANTHROPOL-OGICAL QUARTERLY 41, pp. 49-56.

Fallers, Lloyd and Margaret Fallers
    1976   Sex roles in Edremit. In T.T. Peristiany, ed., MEDITER-RANEAN FAMILY STRUCTURES. Cambridge, England: Cambridge University Press, pp. 243-260.

Feil, D.K.
    1978   Women and men in the Enga tee. AMERICAN ETH-NOLOGIST 5, pp. 263-279.

Fernea, Elizabeth W.
    1969   GUESTS OF THE SHEIK: AN ETHNOGRAPHY OF AN IRAQI VILLAGE. Garden City, N.J.: Anchor Books.

Fernea, Robert A. and Elizabeth Fernea
    1972   Variation in religious observance among Islamic women. In Nikki Keddie, ed., SCHOLARS, SAINTS, AND SUFIS: MUSLIM RELIGIOUS INSTI-TUTIONS IN THE MIDDLE EAST SINCE 1500. Berkeley: University of California Press, pp. 385-401.

Freed, Stanley A. and Ruth S. Freed
    1967   Spirit possession as illness in a North Indian village. In John Middleton, ed., MAGIC, WITCHCRAFT AND CURING. Garden City, NY: Natural History Press, pp. 295-320.

Friedl, Ernestine
    1967a   Dowry and inheritance in modern Greece. In Potter, Diaz, and Foster, eds., PEASANT SOCIETY: A READER. Boston: Little, Brown and Company, pp. 57-62.

    1967b   The position of women: appearance and reality. ANTHROPOLOGICAL QUARTERLY 40, pp. 97-108.

Gamble, S.D.
    1944   A Chinese mutual savings society. FAR EASTERN QUARTERLY 4, pp. 41-52.

Geertz, Clifford
    1962   The rotating credit association: a 'middle rung' in development. ECONOMIC DEVELOPMENT AND CULTURAL CHANGE 10(3), pp. 241-263. Also in

Immanuel Wallerstein, ed., SOCIAL CHANGE: THE COLONIAL SITUATION. New York: Wiley (1966), pp. 420-446.

Goldman, Irving
1961   The Ifugao of the Philippine Islands. In Margaret Mead, ed., CO-OPERATION AND COMPETITION AMONG PRIMITIVE PEOPLES. Boston: Beacon Press, pp. 153-179.

Gomm, R.
1975   Bargaining from weakness: spirit possession on the south Kenya coast. MAN 10, pp. 530-543.

Gonzales, Nancie L.
1976   Multiple migratory experience of Dominican women. ANTHROPOLOGICAL QUARTERLY 49 (1), pp. 36-43.

Goody, Jack and S. J. Tambiah
1973   BRIDEWEALTH AND DOWRY. Cambridge: Cambridge University Press.

Green M.M.
1964   IBO VILLAGE AFFAIRS. New York: Praeger Press.

Hamalian, Arpi
1974   The Shirkets: visiting pattern of Armenians in Lebanon. ANTHROPOLOGICAL QUARTERLY 47(1), pp. 71-92.

√ Harding, Susan
1975   Women and words in a Spanish village. In Rayna R. Reiter, ed., TOWARD AN ANTHROPOLOGY OF WOMEN. New York: Monthly Review Press, pp. 283-308.

Harper, Edward B.
1963   Spirit possession and social structure. In L. K. Bala Ratnam, ed., ANTHROPOLOGY ON THE MARCH. Madras, India: Thompson and Co., pp. 165-197.

Harris, Jack
1939-40   The position of women in a Nigerian society. TRANSACTIONS OF THE NEW YORK ACADEMY OF SCIENCES, II(2). New York: The New York Academy of Sciences, pp. 141-148.

Hay, Margaret Jean
1976   Luo women and economic change during the colonial period. In N. Hafkin and E. Bay, eds., WOMEN IN AFRICA: STUDIES IN SOCIAL AND ECONOMIC CHANGE. Stanford: Stanford University Press, pp. 87-109.

Herskovits, Melville J.
1965 ECONOMIC ANTHROPOLOGY: THE ECONOMIC LIFE OF PRIMITIVE PEOPLES. New York: Norton.

Hewitt, J. N. B.
1932 STATUS OF WOMEN IN IROQUOIS SOCIETY BEFORE 1784. Annual Report of the Board of Regents of the Smithsonian Institution. Washington, D.C.; U.S. Government Printing Office, pp. 475-488.

Hoffer, Carol P. (see also MacCormack)
1974 Madam Yoko: ruler of the Kpa Mende confederacy. In Michelle Rosaldo and Louise Lamphere, eds., WOMAN, CULTURE, AND SOCIETY. Stanford, Calif.: Stanford University Press, pp. 173-187.

1975 Bundu: political implications of female solidarity in a secret society. In Dana Raphael, ed., BEING FEMALE: REPRODUCTION, POWER, AND CHANGE. The Hague: Mouton, pp. 155-163.

Hollander, Nancy C.
1973 Women: the forgotten half. In Pescatello, ed., FEMALE AND MALE IN LATIN AMERICA. Pittsburgh: University of Pittsburgh Press, pp. 141-158.

Holmberg, David H.
n.d. Shamanic sounding: women and bombos among the Tamang of Nepal. n.d., unpublished ms.

Hosekn, Fran P.
1976 WOMEN'S INTERNATIONAL NETWORK NEWS 2(1).

Hussein, Aziza
1965 Voluntary efforts in family planning. Paper presented at the Third Family Planning Conference, Cairo, 16 pp.

1973 The role of the village girl leaders in family planning. Paper presented at the IPPF Regional Seminar, Nicosia, Cyprus, 21 pp.

Huston, Perdita
1979 THIRD WORLD WOMEN SPEAK OUT: INTERVIEWS IN SIX COUNTRIES ON CHANGE, DEVELOPMENT, AND BASIC NEEDS. New York: Published in cooperation with the Overseas Development Council by Praeger.

Hutson, John
1971 A politician in Valloire. In F.G. Bailey, ed., GIFTS AND POISON: THE POLITICS OF REPUTATION. New York: Schocken Books, pp. 69-96.

Ifeka-Moller, Caroline
    1973   "Sitting on a man": Colonialism and the lost political
                institutions of Igbo women: A reply to Judith van Allen.
                CANADIAN JOURNAL OF AFRICAN STUDIES 7(2):
                317-318.

    1977   Female militancy and colonial revolt: the women's war
                of 1929, Eastern Nigeria. In S. Ardener, ed., PER-
                CEIVING WOMEN. New York: John Wiley, (1975)
                pp. 127-157.

Isbell, Billie Jean
    1977   'Those who love me:' an analysis of Andean kinship and
                reciprocity within a ritual context." In R. Bolton and E.
                Mayer, eds., ANDEAN KINSHIP AND MARRIAGE.
                Washington, D.C.: American Anthropological Asso-
                ciation, pp. 81-105.

Jacobson, Doranne
    1974   The women of North and Central India: goddesses and
                wives. In C.J. Matthiasson, ed., MANY SISTERS:
                WOMEN IN CROSS-CULTURAL PERSPECTIVE. New
                York: Macmillan, pp. 99-175.

Jaquette, Jane S.
    1973   Women in revolutionary movements in Latin America.
                JOURNAL OF MARRIAGE AND THE FAMILY 35,
                pp. 344-354.

Jones, David E.
    1972   SANAPIA, COMANCHE MEDICINE WOMAN. New York:
                Holt, Rinehart and Winston.

Joseph, Suad
    1976   Counter-institutions or institutions: structural con-
                straints and potential of women's networks in an urban
                lower class Lebanese neighborhood. Paper presented at
                Conference on Women and Development, Wellesley
                College, 21 pp.

Kaberry, Phyllis
    1952   WOMEN OF THE GRASSFIELDS: A STUDY OF THE
                ECONOMIC POSITION OF WOMEN IN BAMENDA,
                BRITISH CAMEROONS. London: Her Majesty's Station-
                ery Office.

Kandiyoti, Deniz
    1977   Sex roles and social change: a comparative appraisal of
                Turkey's women. SIGNS: JOURNAL OF WOMEN IN
                CULTURE AND SOCIETY 3(1), pp. 57-73.

Katzin, M.F.
    1958   'Partners,' an informal savings institution in Jamaica.
                SOCIAL AND ECONOMIC STUDIES 8, pp. 436-440.

Kiray, Mübeccel
1976a   The new role of mothers: Changing intra-familial rela-
         tionships in a small town in Turkey. In Jean G.
         Peristiany,   ed.,   MEDITERRANEAN   FAMILY
         STRUCTURES.   Cambridge: Cambridge University
         Press, pp. 261-271.

Krige, E. and J. Krige
1943   THE REALM OF THE RAIN-QUEEN. London: Oxford
         University Press.

Kurtz, Donald V.
1973   The rotating credit association: an adaptation to
         poverty. HUMAN ORGANIZATION 32(1), pp. 49-58.

Kurtz, Donald V. and Margaret Showman
1978   The Tanda: a rotating credit association in Mexico.
         ETHNOLOGY 17(1), 65-74.

Lamphere, Louise
1974   Strategies, cooperation, and conflict among women in
         domestic groups.   In Michelle Rosaldo and Louise
         Lamphere, eds.,   WOMAN, CULTURE AND SOCIETY.
         Stanford, Calif.: Stanford University Press, pp. 97-112.

Lasch, Christopher
1978   HAVEN IN A HEARTLESS WORLD: THE FAMILY
         BESIEGED. New York: Basic Books.

Lee, Sea Baick
1976   Village-based family planning in Korea: the case of the
         Mothers' Club.   Paper   presented   at   the
         Conference/Workshop on Non-Formal Education and the
         Rural Poor, Kellogg Center, Michigan State University,
         31 pp.

Leith-Ross, Sylvia
1939   AFRICAN WOMEN: A STUDY OF THE IBO OF
         NIGERIA. London: Faber and Faber, Ltd.

Lerch, Patricia
1977   Spiritual connections and non-local patrons: two dimen-
         sions of female power. Paper presented at the American
         Anthropological Association Annual Meeting.   Houston,
         Texas, November 1977.

Lewis, Barbara
1976   The limitations of group action among entrepreneurs:
         the market women of Abidjan, Ivory Coast. In N. Hafkin
         and E. Bay, eds., WOMEN IN AFRICA: STUDIES IN
         SOCIAL AND ECONOMIC CHANGE. Stanford, Calif.:
         Stanford University Press, pp. 135-156.

Lewis, Ioan M.
1966   Spirit possession and deprivation cults. MAN 1(3), pp. 307-329.

1967   Spirits and the sex war. MAN 2(4), pp. 626-628.

1971   ECSTATIC RELIGION: AN ANTHROPOLOGICAL STUDY OF SPIRIT POSSESSION AND SHAMANISM. Harmondsworth, England: Penguin Books.

1974   Patterns of protest among non-Western women. In R. Prince and D. Barrier, eds., CONFIGURATIONS. The Hague: Mouton, pp. 93-102.

Little, Kenneth
1972   Voluntary associations and social mobility among West African women. CANADIAN JOURNAL OF AFRICAN STUDIES 6(2), pp. 275-288.

1973   AFRICAN WOMEN IN TOWNS: AN ASPECT OF AFRICA'S SOCIAL REVOLUTION. Cambridge, England: Cambridge University Press.

Loeb, E.M.
1934   Patrilineal and matrilineal organization in Sumatra: the Minangkabau. AMERICAN ANTHROPOLOGIST 36(1), pp. 26-56.

Lomnitz, Larissa
n.d.   The role of women in an informal economy. Mimeographed, Mexico, 21 pp.

Luschinsky, Mildred Stroop
1962   THE LIFE OF WOMEN IN A VILLAGE OF NORTH INDIA: A STUDY IN ROLE AND STATUS. Ann Arbor: University Microfilms.

MacCormack, Carol P. (see also Hoffer)
1977   Biological events and cultural control. SIGNS: JOURNAL OF WOMEN IN CULTURE AND SOCIETY 3(1), pp. 93-100.

Maher, Vanessa
1974   Kin, clients, and accomplices: relationships among women in Morocco. In Diana L. Barker and Sheila Allen, eds., SEXUAL DIVISION AND SOCIETY: PROCESS AND CHANGE. London: Tavistock, pp. 52-75.

March, Kathryn S.
1979   THE INTERMEDIACY OF WOMEN: FEMALE GENDER SYMBOLISM AND THE SOCIAL POSITION OF WOMEN AMONG TAMANGS AND SHERPAS OF HIGHLAND NEPAL. Ann Arbor: University Microfilms.

Marsot, Ataf Lufti al-Sayyid
1978   The revolutionary gentlewomen in Egypt. In Beck and Keddie, eds., WOMEN IN THE MUSLIM WORLD. Cambridge, Mass.: Harvard University Press, pp. 261-276.

Mayer, Adrian C.
1963   The significance of quasi-groups in the study of complex societies. In Michael Banton, ed., THE SOCIAL ANTHROPOLOGY OF COMPLEX SOCIETIES. London: Tavistock, pp. 97-122.

McCarthy, Florence E.
1977   Bengali women as mediators of social change. HUMAN ORGANIZATION 36(4), pp. 363-370.

Mintz, Sidney
1971   Men, women, and trade. COMPARATIVE STUDIES IN SOCIETY AND HISTORY 13(3), pp. 247-269.

Mirsky, Jeannette
1961   The Eskimo of Greenland. In Margaret Mead, ed., COOPERATION AND COMPETITION AMONG PRIMITIVE PEOPLES. Boston: Beacon Press, pp. 51-86.

Mohsen, Safia K.
1967   The legal status of women among the Awlad 'Ali. ANTHROPOLOGICAL QUARTERLY 40(3), pp. 153-166.

Morsy, Soheir A.
1978a   Sex roles, power, and illness in an Egyptian village. AMERICAN ETHNOLOGIST 5(1), pp. 137-150.

1978b   Sex differences and folk illness in an Egyptian village. In L. Beck and N. Keddie, eds., WOMEN IN THE MUSLIN WORLD. Cambridge, Mass.: Harvard University Press, pp. 599-619.

Morton, Alice L.
1972-3   SOME ASPECTS OF SPIRIT POSSESSION IN ETHIOPIA. Ph.D. dissertation subject at London School of Economics in Anthropology.

Nadel, Siegfried Frederick
1942   BLACK BYZANTIUM: THE KINGDOM OF NUPE IN

NIGERIA. London: Oxford University Press (For the International African Institute).

Nadim, Nawal al-Messiri
1977   Family relationships in a Harah in Cairo. In Saad Eddin Ibrahim and Nicholas S. Hopkins, eds., ARAB SOCIETY IN TRANSITION: A READER. Cairo: American University in Cairo, pp. 107-120.

Nathanson, C.
1975   Illness and the feminine role: a theoretical review.
            SOCIAL SCIENCE AND MEDICINE 9, pp. 57-62.

✓ Nelson, Cynthia
1971   Self, spirit possession and world view: an illustration
            from Egypt.   INTERNATIONAL JOURNAL OF SOCIAL
            PSYCHIATRY 17, pp. 194-209.

1973   Women and power in nomadic societies of the Middle
            East.   In THE DESERT AND THE SOWN, Institute of
            International Studies, Research Series no. 21.   Berkeley:
            University of California, pp. 43-59.

✓ 1974   Public and private politics: women in Middle Eastern
            World.   AMERICAN ETHNOLOGIST 1(3), pp. 551-563.

Nelson, Nici
1979   Women Must Help Each Other.   In Patricia Caplan and
            Janet M.   Bujra, eds., WOMEN UNITED, WOMEN
            DIVIDED: COMPARATIVE STUDIES OF TEN CONTEM-
            PORARY CULTURES.   Bloomington: Indiana University
            Press, pp. 77-98.

Nerlove, Sara B.
1974   Women's workload and infant feeding practices: a rela-
            tionship with demographic implications.   ETHNOLOGY
            13(2), pp. 207-214.

✓ Netting, Robert McC.
1969   Women's weapons: the politics of domesticity among the
            Kofyar.   AMERICAN   ANTHROPOLOGIST   71(6),
            pp. 1037-1045.

O'Brien, Denise
1977   Female husbands in southern Bantu societies.   In Alice
            Schlegel, ed., SEXUAL STRATIFICATION: A CROSS-
            CULTURAL VIEW.   New York: Columbia University
            Press, pp. 109-126.

Okeyo, Achola Pala
1980   Daughters of the lakes and rivers: colonization and the
            land rights of Luo women. In M. Etienne and E. Leacock,
            eds., WOMEN AND COLONIZATION: ANTHROPO-
            LOGICAL PERSPECTIVES. New York: Praeger Pub-
            lishers, pp. 186-213.

Okonjo, Kamene
1976   The dual-sex political system in operation: Igbo women
            and community politics in midwestern Nigeria.   In N.
            Hafkin and E. Bay, eds., WOMEN IN AFRICA: STUDIES
            IN SOCIAL AND ECONOMIC CHANGE.   Stanford,
            Calif.: Stanford University Press, pp. 45-58.

O'Nell, C. W. and H. A. Selby
 1968   Sex differences in the incidence of susto in two Zapotec
         pueblos: an analysis of the relationship between sex role
         expectations and a folk illness. ETHNOLOGY 7:95-105.

Parsons, Talcott and R. Bales
 1955   FAMILY, SOCIALIZATION AND INTERACTION
         PROCESS. Glencoe, Ill.: Free Press.

Paul, Lois
 1974   The mastery of work and the mystery of sex in a
         Guatemalan village. In Michelle Roaldo and Louise
         Lamphere, eds., WOMAN, CULTURE, AND SOCIETY.
         Stanford, Calif.: Stanford University Press, pp. 281-299.

Paul, Lois and Benjamin D. Paul
 1975   The Mayan midwife as sacred specialist: a Guatemalan
         case. AMERICAN ETHNOLOGIST 2(4), pp. 707-726.

Pignede, Bernard
 1966   LES GURUNGS: UNE POPULATION HIMALAYENNE
         AU NEPAL. Paris: Mouton.

Rahim, Syed A.
 1976   The small group as a medium of communication in a
         rural development program. In G.C. Chu, S.A. Rahim,
         and D.L. Kincaid, eds., COMMUNICATION FOR GROUP
         TRANSFORMATION IN DEVELOPMENT. Honolulu:
         East West Center, East West Communication Institute,
         pp. 145-150.

Randle, Martha C.
 1951   Iroquois women: then and now. In W. Fenton, ed.,
         SYMPOSIUM ON LOCAL DIVERSITY IN IROQUOIS
         CULTURE. Smithsonian Institution, Bureau of Ethnol-
         ogy, Bulletin 149. Washington, D.C.: U.S. Government
         Printing Office, pp. 167-180.

Rapp, Rayna (see also Reiter)
 1979   The new scholarship: review essay in anthropology.
         SIGNS: JOURNAL OF WOMEN IN CULTURE AND
         SOCIETY 4(3), pp. 497-513.

Reiter, Rayna R. (see also Rapp)
 1975   Men and women in the south of France. In Rayna R.
         Reiter, ed., TOWARD AN ANTHROPOLOGY OF
         WOMEN. New York: Monthly Review Press, pp. 252-
         282.

Richards, Cara
 1957   Matriarchy or mistake: The role of Iroquois women
         through time. In Verne F. Ray, ed., CULTURAL
         STABILITY AND CULTURAL CHANGE. Seattle:
         American Ethnological Society, pp. 36-45.

1957   THE ROLE OF IROQUOIS WOMEN: A STUDY OF THE ONONDAGA RESERVATION. Ann Arbor: University Microfilms.

Ritzenthaler, R. E.
1960   Anlu: a women's uprising in the British Cameroons. AFRICAN STUDIES 19(3), pp. 151-156.

Rogers, Everett M. et al.
1976   Network analysis of the diffusion of family planning innovations over time in Korean villages: the role of Mothers' Clubs. In G.C. Chu, S.A. Rahim and D.L. Kincaid, eds., COMMUNICATION FOR GROUP TRANSFORMATION IN DEVELOPMENT. Honolulu: East West Center, East West Communication Institute, pp. 253-276.

Rogers, Susan Carol
1975   Female forms of power and the myth of male dominance: a model of female/male interaction in peasant society. AMERICAN ETHNOLOGIST 2, pp. 741-754.

Romalis, Shelly
1979   Sexual politics and technological change in colonial Africa. Occasional papers in anthropology #1. Buffalo: SUNY Buffalo, pp. 177-187.

Rosaldo, Michelle Zimbalist
1974   Woman, culture, and society: a theoretical overview. In Michelle Rosaldo and Louise Lamphere, eds., WOMAN, CULTURE, AND SOCIETY. Stanford, Calif.: Stanford University Press, pp. 17-42.

1980   SIGNS: JOURNAL OF WOMEN IN CULTURE AND SOCIETY 5 (3), pp. 389-417.

Rosenfeld, Henry
1974   Non-hierarchical, hierarchical and masked reciprocity in an Arab village. ANTHROPOLOGICAL QUARTERLY 47(1), pp. 139-166.

Rubel, A.
1964   The epidemiology of a folk illnes: susto in Hispanic America. ETHNOLOGY 3, pp. 268-283.

Safa, Helen Icken
1976   Class Consciousness Among Working-Class Women in Latin America: Puerto Rico. In June Nash and Helen Icken Safa, eds., SEX AND CLASS IN LATIN AMERICA. New York: Praeger Publishers, pp. 69-85.

Safa, Helen and Brian du Toit (eds.)
1973   MIGRATION AND DEVELOPMENT: IMPLICATIONS
        FOR ETHNIC IDENTITY AND POLITICAL CONFLICT.
        The Hague: Mouton.

Sanday, Peggy R.
1974   Female status in the public domain. In Michelle Rosaldo
        and Louise Lamphere, eds., WOMAN, CULTURE, AND
        SOCIETY. Stanford, Calif.: Stanford University Press,
        pp. 189-206.

Schlegel, Alice
1970   Domestic authority in matrilineal families: a working
        paper. J. STEWARD ANTHROPOLOGICAL SOCIETY
        1(2), pp. 121-128.

1972   MALE DOMINANCE AND FEMALE AUTONOMY: DO-
        MESTIC AUTHORITY IN MATRILINEAL SOCIETIES.
        New Haven: HRAF Press.

Schneider, David and Kathleen Gough (eds.)
1961   MATRILINEAL KINSHIP. Berkeley: University of Cali-
        fornia Press.

Schumacher, Ernst Friedrich
1973   SMALL IS BEAUTIFUL: ECONOMICS AS IF PEOPLE
        MATTERED. New York: Harper and Row.

Sexton, Lorraine Dusak
1980a   From pigs and pearlshells to coffee and cash: socioecon-
        omic change and sex roles in the Daulo Region, Papua,
        New Guinea. Unpublished Ph.D. dissertation, Temple
        University.

1980b   From pigs and pearlshells to coffee and cash: socioecon-
        omic change and sex roles in the Daulo Region, Papua,
        New Guinea. Paper presented at the meeting of the
        Association for Social Anthropology in Oceania,
        Galveston, Texas.

Shack, William
1971   Hunger, anxiety and ritual: deprivation and spirit pos-
        session among the Gurage of Ethiopia. MAN 6, pp. 30-
        43.

Shapiro, Judith
1976   Sexual Hierarchy Among the Yanomana. In June Nash
        and Helen Icken Safa, eds., SEX AND CLASS IN LATIN
        AMERICA. New York: Praeger Publishers, pp. 86-101.

140

Siegel, James
    1978   Curing rites, dreams, and domestic politics in a Sumatran society. GLYPH 3, pp. 18-31.

Simon, Herbert A.
    1969   THE SCIENCES OF THE ARTIFICAL. Cambridge, Mass: MIT Press.

Singh, Sumer
    1974   Co-operatives in Papua New Guinea. NEW GUINEA RESEARCH BULLETIN 58, pp. vii-205.

Smith, Bonnie G.
    1979   Religion and the rise of domesticity: ladies of the Nord. MARXIST PERSPECTIVES, 2(2), pp. 56-82.

✔ Smith, M. Estellie
    1976   Networks and migration resettlement: cherchez la femme. ANTHROPOLOGICAL QUARTERLY 49(1), pp. 20-27.

Stack, Carol
    1974   ALL OUR KIN. New York: Harper and Row.

Staudt, Kathleen A.
    1977   Inequalities in the delivery of services to a female farm clientele: some implications for policy. Discussion paper no. 247. Institute for Development Studies, University of Nairobi.

Steady, Filomina Chioma
    1975   FEMALE POWER IN AFRICAN POLITICS: THE NATIONAL CONGRESS OF SIERRA LEONE. Pasadena, Calif.: California Institute of Technology.

    1976   Protestant women's associations in Freetown, Sierra Leone. In N. Hafkin and E. Bay, eds., WOMEN IN AFRICA: STUDIES IN SOCIAL AND ECONOMIC CHANGE. Stanford: Stanford University Press, pp. 213-237.

✔ Stoler, Ann
   ✔ 1977   Class structure and female autonomy in rural Java. SIGNS: JOURNAL OF WOMEN IN CULTURE AND SOCIETY 3(1), pp. 74-89.

   ✔1977   Rice harvesting in Kali Loro: a study of class and labor in rural Java. AMERICAN ETHNOLOGIST 4(4), pp. 678-698.

Strathern, M.
    1972   WOMEN IN BETWEEN. New York: Seminar Press.

Strobel, Margaret
1976   From <u>lelemama</u> to lobbying: women's associations in Mombasa, Kenya. In N. Hafkin and E. Bay, eds., WOMEN IN AFRICA: STUDIES IN SOCIAL AND ECONOMIC CHANGE. Stanford: Stanford University Press, pp. 183-211.

1979   MUSLIM WOMEN IN MOMBASA, 1890-1975. New Haven: Yale University Press.

Sutton, Constance and Susan Makiesky-Barrow
1977   Social inequality and sexual status in Barbados. In Alice Schlegel, ed., SEXUAL STRATIFICATION: A CROSS-CULTURAL VIEW. New York: Columbia University Press, pp. 292-325.

Tapper, Nancy
1978   The women's subsociety among the Shahsevan nomads of Iran. In Lois Beck and Nikki Keddie, eds., WOMEN IN THE MUSLIN WORLD. Cambridge, Mass.: Harvard University Press, pp. 374-398.

Taqqu, Rachelle
1977   Arab labor in mandatory Palestine, 1920-1948. Unpublished Ph.D. Dissertation, Columbia University.

Taylor, Ellen
1981   WOMEN PARAPROFESSIONALS IN UPPER VOLTA'S RURAL DEVELOPMENT. Ithaca, New York: Rural Development Committee, Cornell University.

Tiffany, Sharon W.
1979   Women, power and the anthropology of politics: a review. INTERNATIONAL JOURNAL OF WOMEN'S STUDIES 2(5), pp. 430-442.

Tinker, Irene
1976   The adverse impact of development on women. In Tinker and Bramsen, eds., WOMEN AND WORLD DEVELOPMENT. Washington, D.C.: American Association for the Advancement of Science, pp. 22-34.

Udy, Stanley H., Jr.
1959   ORGANIZATION OF WORK: A COMPARATIVE ANALYSIS OF PRODUCTION AMONG NONINDUSTRIAL PEOPLES. New Haven, Conn. HRAF Press.

1970   WORK IN TRADITIONAL AND MODERN SOCIETY. Englewood Cliffs, N.J.: Prentice-Hall, Inc.

142

✓ Van Allen, Judith
1972 Sitting on a man: colonialism and the lost political institutions of Igbo women. CANADIAN JOURNAL OF AFRICAN STUDIES 6(2), pp. 165-181.

1976 'Aba Riots' or Igbo 'Women's War'?: ideology, stratification, and the invisibility of women. In N. Hafkin and E. Bay, eds., WOMEN IN AFRICA: STUDIES IN SOCIAL AND ECONOMIC CHANGE. Stanford, Calif.: Stanford University Press, pp. 59-85.

Vatuk, Sylvia
1972 KINSHIP AND URBANIZATION. Berkeley: University of California Press.

Vincent, Joan
1967 AFRICAN ELITE: THE 'BIG MAN' IN A SMALL TOWN. New York: Columbia University Press.

Wallace, Anthony F. C.
1971 Handsome Lake and the decline of the Iroquois matriarchate. In Francis L. K. Hsu, ed., KINSHIP AND CULTURE. Chicago: Aldine Publishing Company, pp. 367-376.

Weiner, Annette B.
1976 WOMEN OF VALUE, MEN OF RENOWN: NEW PERSPECTIVES IN TROBRIAND EXCHANGE. Austin, Texas: University of Texas Press.

Wipper, Audrey (ed.)
1975-6 Rural Women: Development or Underdevelopment? Special edition of RURAL AFRICANA 29 (Winter).

Wiser, William H. and Charlotte Wiser
1963 BEHIND MUD WALLS, 1930-1960. Berkeley: University of California Press.

Wolf, Eric R.
1963 Kinship, friendship, and patron-client relations in complex societies. In M. Banton, ed., THE SOCIAL ANTHROPOLOGY OF COMPLEX SOCIETIES. London: Tavistock Publications, pp. 1-22.

Wolf, M.
1972 WOMEN AND THE FAMILY IN RURAL TAIWAN. Stanford: Stanford University Press.

Yanagisako, Sylvia Junko
1977 Women-centered networks in urban bilateral kinship. AMERICAN ETHNOLOGIST 4(4), pp. 207-226.

Young, A.
1975 Why Amhara get <u>Kureynya</u>: sickness and possession in an Ethiopian <u>Zar</u> cult. AMERICAN ETHNOLOGIST 2(3), pp. 576-584.

Young, Michael and Peter Willmott
1962 FAMILY AND KINSHIP IN EAST LONDON. Middlesex: Penguin Books

Index

152